VW
NEW BEETLE
Performance Handbook

Keith Seume

MBI Publishing Company

First published in 2001 by MBI Publishing Company, Galtier Plaza, Suite 200, 380 Jackson Street, St. Paul, MN 55101-3885, USA.

MBI Publishing Company books are also available at discounts in bulk quantity for industrial or sales-promotional use. For details write to Special Sales Manager at Motorbooks International Wholesalers & Distributors, Galtier Plaza, Suite 200, 380 Jackson Street, St. Paul, MN 55101-3885, USA.

Library of Congress Cataloging-in-Publication Data Available

ISBN 0-7603-0909-4

On the front cover
Radical New Beetle from Classics by Bernt captured in all its glory by Didier Soyeux of *Super GTI Magazine.*

On the title page
Dietrich-built New Beetle features Kerscher rims which measure 9x18 at the front and a massive 11x18 at the rear! Tires are 235/40 and 265/35 Continentals. *Super GTI Magazine*

On the back cover
Autobahn Designs' beautiful project car is based on a 2000 1.8-liter Turbo and has been kitted out with bodywork by Bernt.

Edited by: Sara Perfetti
Designed by: Dan Poppie

Printed in China

Contents

	Foreword	5
CHAPTER 1	History	6
CHAPTER 2	Overview	16
CHAPTER 3	Engines	28
CHAPTER 4	Transmission	42
CHAPTER 5	Suspension, Brakes, Wheels, and Tires	46
	upgrading the front suspension	58
	upgrading the rear suspension	65
CHAPTER 6	Bodywork	72
	winging your beetle	82
	beetle splitters	86
CHAPTER 7	Interiors	90
APPENDIX A	Specifications	104
APPENDIX B	Specialists	116
	Index	126

Dedication

To J. C. Mays and Freeman Thomas,
without whom there would be no
New Beetle.

Foreword

No other car in recent history has created so much media interest—for all the right reasons, I hasten to add—as the New Beetle. In fact, there probably hasn't been a car since the original air-cooled Beetle that has generated so great a following in such a short space of time.

Across the United States and Europe, television networks broadcast images of VW's new baby from the Detroit Auto Show on prime time TV—a scenario quite unheard of before. Every manufacturer, from General Motors to Hyundai, releases new models each year, but how many of those receive major media attention? Right from the very start, it seems, the New Beetle was destined to become a cult car.

When it first hit the dealerships, supplies of the New Beetle could not keep pace with demand. There were tales of arguments between customers as to who was first to put their money down on the red sedan in the corner. Some dealers even demanded a premium over the list price to guarantee delivery of this precious commodity. Volkswagen had never had it so good.

However, even though excitement was running at fever pitch, few people could ever have expected the New Beetle to become the center of an industry dedicated to improving the performance, handling, and appearance of an already excellent product. But no sooner had the New Beetle hit the street than a whole host of aftermarket specialists began offering wings, wheels, and accessories for VW's fun car, followed swiftly by engine conversions, brake upgrades and suspension kits. Herbie's kid brother had suddenly "all growed up. . . ."

I was fortunate to be one of the earliest British journalists, if not the first, to drive the New Beetle, getting behind the wheel of a preproduction model in the United States several months ahead of full-scale production. Until then, I had regarded the New Beetle as something of a diversion that couldn't possibly solve the many problems from which Volkswagen appeared to be suffering at the time. Sales of VW products had not been good, and pressure from Far-Eastern rivals meant that the

German company was struggling. But, as soon as I jumped behind the wheel of the New Beetle, I realized this was a great car in its own right—one that deserved to succeed and one that, surely, was going to thrust Volkswagen back into the limelight.

Today, the New Beetle is the car to be seen in and, just like its air-cooled predecessor, it is a totally classless car. Adopted by secretaries and socialites alike as the car of choice, the popularity of the New Beetle can only go from strength to strength. With the help of this book, I hope you will be inspired to turn your New Beetle into something a little more individual—a car that will guarantee you more smiles per mile than any other you are ever likely to own.

Many people have helped with the production of this book, and I must say a special word of thanks to certain of them: Tim Hildabrand (New Dimensions), for providing so many great images and such useful information; Dave Anderson (Autobahn Designs), who has been extremely helpful from the first day I wandered into his shop a few years ago; Ralph Hollack (Autotech); Greg Woo (Neuspeed); Quaife Engineering; Didier Soyeux (Super GTI magazine) in France, for access to his photo files; likewise Dean Kirsten (Hot VWs magazine), in the United States; Volkswagen USA, for the use of a 1.8 Turbo New Beetle while conducting research; Volkswagen AG, for access to the factory photographic files; Brian Burrows, for lending me the first New Beetle in the UK; Luke Theochari (Terry's Beetle Services), for the body kit how-tos; Volksline, for the suspension how-to; Darrell Vittone (Techtonics Tuning), for inspiring me to cross the seemingly great divide from air-cooled to water-cooled engineering. To the many others who have assisted with this project, I say a big "thank you."

I must also, of course, thank John Adams-Graf at MBI Publishing Company for his patience with this long-overdue project and my dear wife, Gwynn, for her help and support along the way.

—Keith Seume
Cornwall, England

Chapter 1

History

When it was launched in 1998, the New Beetle captured the hearts of the American people. For many, it rekindled memories of a love affair with the original VW Beetle that began way back in the 1950s. *Volkswagen*

When the doors were flung open at the 1994 North American International Auto Show at Detroit, nobody—not even the most seasoned automotive journalist or industry expert—was prepared for the stunning styling exercise displayed on the Volkswagen stand. There, among the well-established Golf, Jetta, and Passat models sat a quite sensational bug-like vehicle that aroused more than a few memories of the good old VW Beetle.

This was Concept 1, the undoubted star of the Auto Show and proof that Volkswagen had what it takes to stop people dead in their tracks. Few show cars in recent history have generated such media interest and even fewer have made it into production. Concept 1 made people sit up and think: "See, modern cars don't have to all look the same! Cars can be fun." For Volkswagen, it was the shot in the arm the company needed, for competition in the North American market had never been so tough.

The two people responsible for this exciting new styling exercise were Freeman Thomas and J. Carrol Mays, both of whom had studied at the American Art Center College of Design.

After graduating, they crossed the Atlantic Ocean, Mays to join Audi's styling department, Thomas finding his niche at Porsche. However, in 1991, they made the return journey to California to open Volkswagen's new American Design Center at Simi Valley.

Thomas and Mays were aware that, after years of suffering at the hands of the Far Eastern manufacturers, VW needed something to pull people back into the dealerships. It needed a car that would make people sit up and take notice, a car that would put a smile on their faces—a car with soul. Volkswagen's own engineers had already spent several years and millions of Deutschmarks on developing a new city car known by the project name of Chico. This was to have been a subcompact model designed to slot into the European model range below the highly successful Polo. Indeed, the Chico was on the verge of going into production when the decision was made to call a halt, as it was considered commercially unviable to continue. The project cost Volkswagen dearly, not only in financial terms but also in loss of prestige. What Volkswagen needed was a new

diversion—something to draw the public gaze away from past problems. Something to put VW back on the map.

Freeman Thomas and J. C. Mays were well aware of Volkswagen's predicament. They felt the company needed a little light relief in the form of a car with something of the timeless charm of the original Beetle—a car that would attract attention from the media and public alike. When launched at the 1994 Detroit Auto Show, Concept 1 certainly had the desired effect, although it wasn't expected to be viewed as anything other than a styling exercise. Indeed, Volkswagen management appeared to regard the cheeky little bug-like vehicle as nothing more than a ploy to attract attention to the show-stand. Or did they?

Nobody seemed quite ready for the overwhelming enthusiasm with which Concept 1 was greeted on its unveiling at Detroit. Rival manufacturers looked on in dismay as Volkswagen stole the limelight; automotive journalists waxed lyrical about this amazing little car, which hinted at Volkswagen's past; the public simply demanded to know when it was going to be on

From the very beginning, the Concept 1 project (which later developed into the New Beetle) was seen as a way to put some fun back into motoring. This early sketch likened Concept 1 to a kid's toy. *Volkswagen*

The first design sketches showed a very rounded, Beetle-like car with many design references to the original air-cooled Beetle, such as running boards and grilles below the headlights. *Volkswagen*

At the rear, there were even suggestions that the old Beetle's air vents below the rear window might be incorporated into the design, although this idea was never followed through. *Volkswagen*

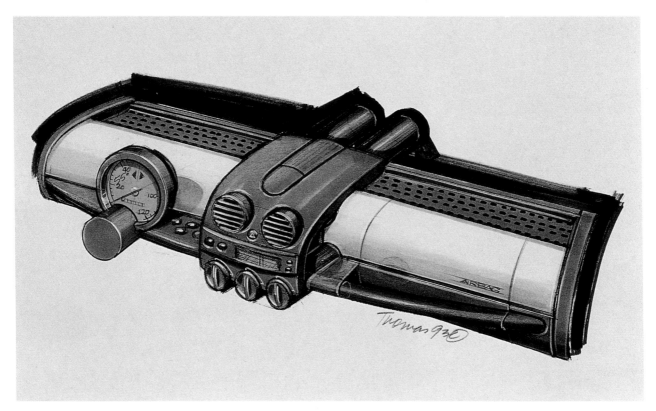

A great deal of thought was given to the design of Concept 1's dashboard. Many of the elements seen here, such as the large speedometer, were later incorporated into the final design. *Volkswagen*

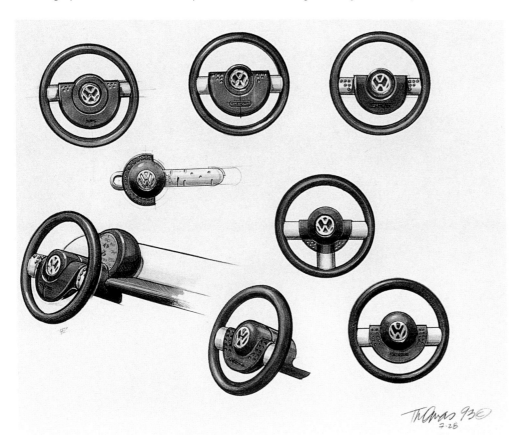

Many hours were spent attending to every detail in the quest for perfection. Who would ever have thought that designing a steering wheel would require so much effort? *Volkswagen*

As Concept 1 began to take shape on the drawing board, certain basic design elements were agreed upon at an early stage, including the use of separate fenders and large-diameter wheels. *Volkswagen*

Only when dozens of drawings had been made was the design turned into a three-dimensional model, bringing Concept 1 to life. *Volkswagen*

sale. That question remained unanswered throughout the show, with senior Volkswagen management simply smiling and saying nothing. The reason for the apparent air of secrecy was that nobody really knew what the future would be for Concept 1. It was all very much a case of "wait and see."

In the wake of the Detroit Auto Show, it was clear that Concept 1 had struck the right chord with the media, and there was talk of limited production at some point in the future, but nothing was certain. However, public reaction was stronger than anyone could have expected and, following the show, Volkswagen dealerships across America were besieged with customers demanding to know when this new "Beetle" would be available. It is ironic that for years Volkswagen had apparently turned its back on the original Beetle, yet it took a styling exercise inspired by the original car to bring people back into the showrooms.

Mays and Thomas felt that the old Beetle stood for certain virtues that appeared to have been forgotten in the rush to build ever more efficient automobiles: simplicity, reliability, honesty, and originality. Customers viewed new cars as being far from simple, the underhood scene being dominated by complex electrical systems and sophisticated engine-management modules. Likewise, modern cars may be statistically reliable, but their complexity means that only a skilled mechanic has any chance of fixing one by the roadside. Honest?

Public scepticism at the claims made by the major manufacturers was running at an all-time high. Original? To many people, it was difficult, if not impossible, to tell one car from another out on the freeway, unless you were close enough to read the badge. Modern cars, designed by computer and built by robots, all look the same.

A year after Concept 1 appeared at Detroit, Volkswagen unleashed another surprise on an already stunned world: At the 1995 Geneva show, a bright red Concept 1 cabriolet was displayed alongside the original yellow sedan. This acted as a catalyst for more public demands about when such a vehicle was going to become available, yet Volkswagen still remained noncommittal about the whole project. It was to be a whole year before the company finally gave in to public demand and announced that, yes, a new car based on the Concept 1 styling exercise would indeed be built by the end of the century.

To help gauge public demand in the United States, Volkswagen set up a free-access telephone line to allow members of the public to express their thoughts about the new car. The phone line was soon overwhelmed with calls, mostly from people saying: "You build it, I'll buy it!" While the reaction may have come as something of a shock to senior VW management, for Freeman and Thomas it was simply proof that their efforts had not been in vain.

Following the rapturous welcome Concept 1 received at the Detroit show in January 1994, Volkswagen once again stunned the automotive world by displaying a Concept 1 cabriolet-styling mockup at the Geneva motor show the following year. *Volkswagen*

11

Work on the Concept 1 project continued, with further redesigns of the front end. This drawing, which dates back to 1995, shows a front bumper that closely resembles that of the final New Beetle design. *Volkswagen*

A full-size clay model allowed the design team to finalize the styling. *Volkswagen*

From the outset, Concept 1 was intended to be a thoroughly modern vehicle, despite its retro styling, and an important part of the whole concept was the drivetrain. Unlike its forebear, the new sedan would have front-wheel drive. A variety of powertrains were considered, including a technologically fascinating "hybrid" part-gas, part-electric motor, a 1.9-liter turbo diesel, and an all-electric version. Also under consideration at the time was the use of the European Polo floorpan assembly, to save production costs.

However, later in 1995, Volkswagen showed another prototype at the Japan Motor Show, this time clearly based on the larger Golf floorpan, with its longer wheelbase and greater range of drivetrain options, including the VR6 and 2-liter fuel-injected gasoline engines. The front suspension would be by MacPherson strut, the rear by Volkswagen's well-proven torsion-beam axle, similar to that developed for the Golf range over 20 years earlier. Sixteen-inch wheels were chosen, in preference to the huge 18-inch diameter rims seen on the original Concept 1, to allow sufficient suspension travel within the closely fitting fenders. Mays and Freeman felt that large-diameter wheels and tires

In October 1995, Volkswagen displayed this almost-production-ready prototype at the Tokyo show. It was at this show that Volkswagen announced that the new car would be called the New Beetle. *Volkswagen*

In January 1999, Volkswagen showed its sensational New Beetle RSi project, a high-performance road car, christened by some "Herbie on Steroids." *Dean Kirsten*

Even the engine of the RSi prototype looked out of this world. Six-cylinder, turbocharged, and mated to a six-speed transmission, the engine was as stylish as the exterior. *Dean Kirsten*

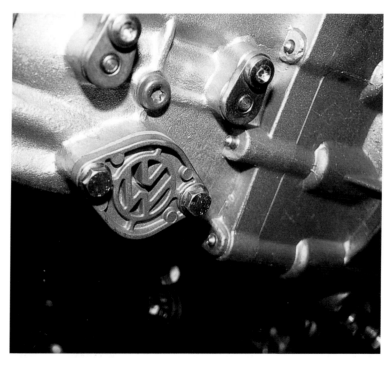

One fun detail on the New Beetle that only the repair shop is ever likely to see is this tiny VW logo on a cover plate on the underside of the 2-liter gasoline engine. *Author*

not only resulted in improved ride characteristics but also gave the vehicle an air of quality. After all, you never see Rolls-Royces on 13-inch wheels.

While the drivetrain may have been thoroughly modern, the external styling was clearly inspired by the original Beetle. Several design references brought back memories of that familiar friend, not the least of which were the seemingly separate fenders, sloping hood, and "running boards" below the doors. The headlamps, too, mimicked those of the original Beetle, sloping and following the contours of the front fenders. Below them were two air vents which resembled the horn grilles of the old car. At the rear, large round taillights looked uncannily similar to the big "elephant's foot" lights featured on the late-model Super Beetles. Even the single exhaust tailpipe had something of the original look about it, poking, as it did, through the rear apron.

In profile, Concept 1 looked uncannily like the Beetle of old, with its high, domed roof and gently curved fenders—but any similarity stopped there, for this new design no longer sported separate chromed bumpers, polished side trim, chromed hub caps, flat windshield, or even quarter-lights in the door windows.

From any angle, the New Beetle is stylish. It is also instantly recognizable, even by those who have no real interest in automobiles. It is truly unique. *Super GTI Magazine*

Inside the prototypes were a number of design references to the earlier car, including a large speedometer located directly in front of the driver, a passenger grab-handle on the dashboard, and another pair of assist handles on the door pillars for the use of the rear-seat passengers. There was even a small vase on the dashboard, reminiscent of the accessory "bud vases" so popular among VW owners in the 1950s. However, no old Beetle owner would recognize the comfortable, supportive seats with their integral headrests, the air bags, or the deep dashboard with its built-in radio and matching center console. Looking beneath the skin, there were side-impact bars, crumple-zones front and rear, and rollover protection built into the roof.

At the Japanese show, over a year since the car's first apperance, Volkswagen finally announced the name of this exciting model: the New Beetle. The response from VW enthusiasts was mixed; many believed that the name "Beetle" was sacred and should only ever be used in connection with the original air-cooled sedan—others simply smiled and recalled fond memories of an earlier love affair with VW's funny little Bug.

It would be almost two years before Volkswagen finally shipped New Beetles, built at its plant in Mexico, to its dealerships in the United States, and several months more before offering them for sale in Europe. To begin with, demand for the car far outstripped supply. Dealers across the United States told tales of customers outbidding each other in an effort to be the first on their block to own one of VW's new toys. The enthusiasm would continue unabated for several more months until, eventually, VW stepped up production to cope with the unprecedented demand.

It was not long before the aftermarket industry took advantage of this frenzy of interest in the New Beetle and offered wheel and tire packages, suspension kits, and various glass-fiber add-ons. It appeared that, just like its predecessor, the New Beetle had been taken to heart by the whole world.

Chapter 2

Overview

When the New Beetle first appeared on the market in 1998, it had a dramatic effect on the whole automotive scene. At last, here was a car that put the fun back into motoring and, for once, it was not the product of some low-volume manufacturer with an exotic-sounding name but the prodigy of one of the best-known names in the automobile world: Volkswagen.

The New Beetle immediately rekindled memories of seemingly far-off days, when people drove their cars for no other reason than to have a good time. Forget the price of crude oil on the world market, forget the pressures from the "Greens"—get out in your car and enjoy! The New Beetle put a smile on everyone's face.

Of course, there were immediate attempts to compare the New Beetle with its long-lost spiritual "brother," the original Volkswagen Bug, but such comparisons are, in truth, meaningless—unless you wish to ignore 60 years of progress and heaven only knows how many millions of dollars of investment, not to mention a rapidly changing world in which emissions and rising gas prices dominate the conversation. No, like it or not, the New Beetle was no new Beetle. It was, and is, a car in its own right with its own identity and its own sense of purpose. This is a new car for a new age.

The New Beetle shares no components with its predecessor. It is a front-engined, front-wheel-drive "hatchback" with all the features one comes to

At the original press presentations, held first in Detroit and then throughout the world, the New Beetle was the subject of unparalleled media attention. Super GTI Magazine

Even though the New Beetle was designed to put a smile on your face, it still meets even the most stringent safety requirements. This cut-away display vehicle shows just how. *Super GTI Magazine*

Initially there was a relatively restricted choice of models available to the would-be New Beetle buyer, but Volkswagen soon let it be known that more advanced versions, such as this Europe-only V5-engined example, were to follow. *Volkswagen*

As if a five-cylinder New Beetle isn't enough, how about Volkswagen's wild New Beetle RSi? Six-speed, six-cylinders, and more wings than a Formula One car. Awesome! *Volkswagen*

Under the skin, the New Beetle is, in fact, based on the drivetrain of Volkswagen's Golf and Jetta 4 models. Front-wheel-drive layout allows maximum use of interior space. *Volkswagen*

Even though the floorpan and drivetrain are shared with the Golf and Jetta, the New Beetle is potentially the best-handling car of the trio, as its body shell is far more rigid, largely thanks to those thick windshield pillars. *Volkswagen*

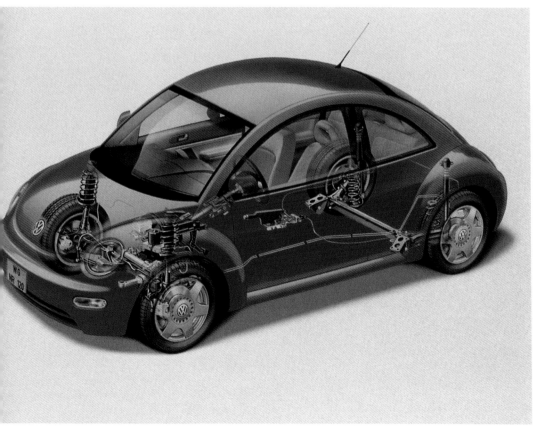

MacPherson strut front suspension and rack-and-pinion steering make for sharp handling. At the rear, Volkswagen's trademark torsion-beam axle keeps things simple. *Volkswagen*

Step inside the New Beetle and you're immediately reminded that driving this car is meant to be a fun experience. Large, single gauge pod mounted in front of the driver is reminiscent of the original Beetle's dash layout. *Volkswagen*

What other modern car sports a flower vase on the dashboard? The answer to that question is simple: none! The New Beetle puts the fun back into motoring. *Volkswagen*

associate with modern cars, including fuel injection, air conditioning, antilock brakes, and air bags. Indeed, safety is a main priority in the New Beetle, with an advanced passenger protection system that includes complex energy-absorbing crumple zones, passenger and driver air bags, side-impact protection, self-tensioning seat belts, front and rear headrests, and an extremely strong body shell that has proved to offer excellent rollover protection.

Although the New Beetle is, as far as the dealers are concerned, a new car, in technological terms it can be considered a development of the well-proven Volkswagen Golf. How's that? Because the New Beetle shares its platform—the buzz-word for what everyone used to know as the chassis—with the top-selling European Golf Mk 4, making it one of the best-engineered new cars on the market. (To give the Mk4 platform its in-house designation, it's A4, but don't confuse this with Audi's A4 model.) The A4 models (which include the Jetta sedan) are among the most respected models in their fields, and justly so. They have proved to be built to high standards and have an excellent track record on reliability and safety.

A4 Platform

The A4 platform features MacPherson strut front suspension along with a torsion-beam rear axle that incorporates an anti-roll (sway) bar and trailing arms. This axle is attached to the frame with Volkswagen's so-called "track-correcting bushings," which are designed to minimize "rear steering" brought on as a result of suspension deflection. Coil springs with separate shock absorbers provide the suspension medium at the rear. The thinking behind this is that by separating the springs from the shocks, significantly less road noise would be transmitted to the interior.

Braking is provided by servo-assisted discs at all four corners, those at the front being ventilated for improved heat dissipation. From 1999, all models were equipped with anti-lock braking (ABS) for increased safety, a feature previously only available as an option in some markets. Servo-assistance means that pedal pressure is kept to a minimum at all times, although there is still plenty of "feel" for the driver. Despite this, the brakes of a New Beetle are one area that enthusiasts generally feel is ripe for further improvement. Steering is by power-assisted rack and pinion, with approximately 3.2 turns lock to lock.

Wheels are either steel with full-size plastic covers or six-spoke cast aluminum, the latter being optional on certain models but standard equipment on the top-of-the-range turbo New Beetles. In all instances they are shod with 205/55x16 H-rated all-season radial tires.

Drivetrain

When the New Beetle was first introduced, two engine packages were available: a 2.0-liter four-cylinder gasoline unit and a 1.9-liter turbo-diesel. In 1999 the range was expanded to include a 1.8-liter turbo gasoline engine, which has attracted much favorable comment. In Europe, a 1,600-cc engine was even launched during the year 2000, aimed at the budget end of the market, although this would not be a logical starting point for any performance modifications. Do you remember the old adage: "There ain't no substitute for cubic inches"? Well, some things may have changed in the world of automotive technology but this little saying still tends to hold true where the New Beetle is concerned. For 2001, Volkswagen clearly thought about this and announced certain markets would be treated to the launch of a 2.3-liter V5-engined New Beetle, producing 170 horsepower, followed soon after by the mighty 3.2-liter VR6-engined New Beetle RSi!

The eight-valve 2.0-liter engine produces 115 horsepower (85kW) at 5,200 rpm and 122 ft-lb (165Nm) of torque at 2,600 rpm. By comparison, the 1.9 TDI engine produces just 90 horsepower (66kW) at 3,750 rpm but an impressive 155 ft-lb (210Nm) of torque at a lowly 1,900 rpm. However, the 20-valve 1.8-liter turbocharged gasoline engine punches out 150 horsepower (110kW) at 5,800 rpm and a sensational 162 ft-lb (220Nm) of torque all the way from 2,200 rpm to 4,200 rpm. A torque-curve as flat as that of the 1.8 turbo guarantees plenty of driving fun on the open road. The 170-horsepower 2.3-liter V5 engine gives the New Beetle true 120-mile-per-hour capability but, impressive though this is, it is humbled by the 225 horsepower VR6 RSi—that is capable of almost 140 miles per hour and can accelerate from 0 to 60 miles per hour in 6.5 seconds!

Coupled to these engines (with the exception of the RSi) is a choice of either a cable-shifted five-speed manual transmission or an optional four-speed electronically controlled fully automatic gearbox. Incidentally, models with manual transmissions cannot be started unless the clutch pedal is first pushed to the floor, a safety feature designed to prevent owners from attempting to start the car while in gear. Clutch operation is hydraulic on all manual New Beetles.

In order to extract the best from each engine package, the drivetrain ratios vary from model to model. The final drive ratio of the turbo-dicsel is the highest (i.e., numerically the lowest) at 3.39:1, followed by that of the turbo gasoline model at 3.94:1 and then the nonturbo gasoline version at 4.24:1. In addition, there are variations between models in terms of the internal gear ratios to take into account the different power and torque characteristics of each engine.

The RSi comes with all-wheel-drive courtesy of Volkswagen's high-tech "4-Motion" drivetrain, complete with Haldex electronically controlled clutch system. The RSi also features a six-speed gearbox.

Body and Interior

The New Beetle is built to exacting standards, a fact borne out by close examination of a finished car. The door gaps and general panel fit are superb, unlike those of many rival products from the U.S. or Far Eastern manufacturers. This is partly due to Volkswagen's use of the latest laser-welding techniques, which result in a body shell of unmatchable rigidity.

But for all its underlying technology, it is the overall appearance of the New Beetle that grabs people's attention first of all. The cute, rounded lines are unique. There are no separate bumpers to spoil the lines: the all-enveloping front and rear deformable panels flow seamlessly into the fenders and hood. The New Beetle can be considered a classic shape only in that it is timeless in its simplicity—in all other respects it is a thoroughly modern design. Forget those comparisons with the old Bug: we are talking here about a car for the

Anyone who ever drove one of the original VW Bugs will remember this little detail—the rear passenger grab-handle reappeared on the New Beetle as part of the retro design. *Volkswagen*

If the New Beetle has a shortcoming it's that the trunk space is slightly limited. However, the hatchback design and folding rear seats make it a practical everyday car. *Volkswagen*

The 2-liter gasoline engine produces 115 horsepower at 5,200 rpm and 122 ft-lb of torque at 2,600 rpm. It is an excellent engine with a heritage that stretches back to the 1970s. *Volkswagen*

The 1.9-liter turbo-diesel injection engine may only produce 90 horsepower at 3,750 rpm, but what it lacks in power it makes up for in torque: How about 155 ft-lb at just 1,900 rpm? *Volkswagen*

Most impressive of the four-cylinder production engines is the 20-valve 1.8-liter turbo gasoline motor. It punches out 150 horsepower at 5,800 rpm and 162 lb-ft of torque all the way from 2,200 to 4,200 rpm! *Volkswagen*

The 170-horsepower 2.3-liter V5 engine gives the New Beetle true 120-mile-per-hour capability. Put simply, the V5 engine is a VR6 Golf motor with one cylinder lopped off. *Super GTI Magazine*

Year 2000 saw the launch in Europe of a 1.6-liter New Beetle designed to cut fuel costs to the bone. Maybe not the first choice for the sporting driver, but a fun car all the same. *Volkswagen*

twenty-first century. The flush-mounted, lightweight light units back and front emphasize the modernity of its styling, the headlamps incorporating the latest projector-beam halogen lighting components, which are a million miles from the old Bug's candle-powered six-volt glow-worms.

As we take a look inside the New Beetle, we discover a number of design references to the past, including the inclusion of a pair of rear-passenger assist straps, rather like those found in the original Bug. There is also a large passenger grab-handle on the dashboard, just like the one on the old Beetle, and even a whimsical "bud vase" in which to place your favorite flower. (Any flower will do, but a daisy is the preferred choice!)

Ahead of the driver, a large round instrument display includes the speedometer, a tiny tachometer, fuel gauge, and a temperature gauge. The whole display is illuminated at night by a soft blue light, complemented by eye-catching red needles. This striking blue-with-red theme is carried throughout the whole driver display, including the heater controls and the factory-fitted radio. Silver accents on the steering

wheel, gear lever, and handbrake are designed to add to the sense of fun by suggesting the use of high-tech billet aluminum, when, in fact, the components are largely made of plastic.

Probably the one feature that immediately strikes any first-time driver of a New Beetle as being rather unusual is the depth of the dashboard, from the steering wheel to the windshield. In most cars, the driver is quite capable of wiping the windshield glass, should the need arise. In a New Beetle, this is quite out of the question, as the windshield slopes away to the rear edge of the short hood. At first, this can be quite off-putting, as the driver has the impression that the front of the car is much longer than it really is. However, after a few miles of driving, this "problem" soon disappears, and the driver sits back to enjoy the New Beetle experience.

In all other areas, the New Beetle's interior is, truth be told, very much like that of most other small modern cars, if a little more colorful. The seats are comfortable and provide plenty of support for passengers on a longer journey, and access to the rear is made simple by an ingenious spring-loaded hinge mechanism on the front seat backs. Rear headroom is, it has to be said, severely limited by

Mighty 225-horsepower six-cylinder New Beetle RSi can rocket from 0 to 60 in a shade over six seconds and reach a top speed of 140 miles per hour. Now that sounds like fun! *Volkswagen*

the shape of the heavy, curved rear roof pillars, which are a consequence of the New Beetle's profile.

Trunk space is compromised, too, largely due to the angular corners of the rear hatchback. This, combined with a rather high rear loading sill, means that access to the trunk can be slightly awkward when trying to load heavy or bulky items of luggage. Unless care is exercised, it will be only a matter of time before the paintwork around the rear hatch becomes scuffed. In terms of luggage capacity, the New Beetle isn't overendowed, with just 12 cubic feet of space available. However, this can be increased considerably by folding down the rear seatbacks.

On the Open Road

So, you've taken the bait and decided to get behind the wheel of a New Beetle? But which one? The three basic models (2.0-liter gasoline, 1.8-liter turbo, and 1.9-liter turbo-diesel) all promise a fun driving experience but are very different in character.

The most down-to-earth model is, without doubt, the original 2.0-liter gasoline-engined New Beetle, with its relatively modest 115-horsepower four-cylinder eight-valve motor. The engine is not renowned for its smoothness, and it has a distinctly raw edge to it when pushed hard through the rev range. However, it is a willing engine, and one that gives the New Beetle genuine 100-mile-per-hour capability. (When the conditions allow, as they say!) Drivers will find that models with manual transmission have a delightfully light gear change, which is just as well, as you need to take full advantage of the gearbox to extract the best performance from the car. This is not to say that the 2.0-liter lacks power or has a narrow power band, but you have to remember that outright performance was not a priority when the car was designed.

Other considerations, such as fuel economy and passenger comfort, had a far higher priority, meaning that the car feels high-geared and a little lacking in sparkle. The automatic models suffer from this far more, as one might expect. Any car with automatic transmission will invariably feel a little sluggish alongside a comparable manual version, and the New Beetle is no exception here. However, again bearing in mind the anticipated use, the automatic New Beetle is a fine car that undoubtedly appeals to urban drivers or those with a desire to take life a little easier.

Stepping up to the turbo-diesel model, the 1.9 TDI, there is an immediate difference when the engine is started—the engine note! Any diesel-engined car will sound "clattery" at idle, especially when cold. It is part and parcel of the diesel's character and something that you either accept or dislike—but things are changing. Diesels have long had a bad reputation among more sporting drivers, largely because in the past diesel-engined cars tended to be slow, noisy, and smelly. Today's new breed of turbo-diesel, however, will come as something of a revelation to anyone unfamiliar with the latest technology. Gone is the sluggish performance and the truck-like rattle. In their place is performance that is the match of many gasoline-powered cars and a smoothness that has to be experienced to be believed. Only at the gas station, where diesel pumps are often shared with truckers, does the reality hit home: diesel fuel smells!

Out on the open road, the 1.9 TDI New Beetle is a delight, with sparkling performance and a most amazing spread of torque that tempts you to leave it in fifth gear and let the engine do the work. Even the engine note, when pressed hard, has a certain appeal, for it sounds powerful and quite unlike any regular diesel. The only thing a diesel engine won't do is rev high, so it is natural to have to make full use of the gearbox when accelerating hard from rest.

If sporting pretensions are not your main priority, you could do far worse than consider an automatic TDI New Beetle, as the added torque of the diesel engine more than compensates for the power losses through the transmission. The pick of the litter, though, is undoubtedly the 1.8T turbo-gasoline New Beetle, with its high-tech five-valve-per-cylinder 1,781-cc engine, which produces a very useful 150 horsepower. This is the same basic unit chosen by Audi for use in its sensational TT coupe and roadster, an engine that readily lends itself to upgrading. Indeed, in the Audi TT, one version produces 225 horsepower (DIN).

It is a smooth engine with plenty of urge, even from relatively low revs. It turns the New Beetle from a pussycat into a full-grown tiger at the push of the gas pedal, with seemingly never-ending torque once the turbo comes on boost. If there is a

flaw, it's that there is very little sense of urgency at low revs (most noticeable at less than 2,000 rpm), meaning that full use needs to be made of the gearbox if optimum performance is to be achieved.

All New Beetles feel stable at speed, the 1.8 Turbo in particular, thanks largely to the electrically operated roof spoiler, which deploys at approximately 100 miles per hour. Unlike its famous forebear, the New Beetle is little troubled by cross-winds; the weight of the drivetrain over the front wheels helping to keep the nose firmly planted on the road. In common with all modern cars, the New Beetle, which has been designed with stylish good looks as a first priority, has benefited from a great deal of wind tunnel development, the net result being a coefficient of drag (Cd) of just 0.38.

Why is a low Cd figure so important? Because aerodynamic drag influences performance and gas mileage. Relatively recently, to achieve 100-mile-per-hour performance, manufacturers had to fit large-capacity engines to their cars because the drag coefficients were so high. As for gas mileage—who even gave it a second thought?

In common with the majority of modern front-wheel-drive cars, the New Beetle has what can best be described as very safe handling characteristics. When driven fast into a corner, there is little chance of spinning off into the undergrowth, as might be the case with a high-powered rear-wheel-drive car. This is because the New Beetle has a natural tendency to understeer—where the front of the car will tend to run wide on a bend, as opposed to oversteer where the rear of the vehicle will want to step out of line.

If the New Beetle has one fault, it is that its suspension is typically German—by that we mean that it has relatively firm springs (giving what at first sight appears to be a stiff, sporting ride) but soft damping. This combination is fine for long spell on the freeway but will mean that the car tends to wallow on long fast bends. The New Beetle also leans quite dramatically when pushed hard into a bend, partly as a consequence of soft damping and partly due to the use of relatively soft anti-roll (sway) bars.

As a whole, the New Beetle is a fine-handling car and one that can be hustled along at quite a high rate of knots when conditions allow. However, as with all mass-production cars, there is room for improvement, as we hope to show.

So, there we have it: the New Beetle. A car for the twenty-first century with much to offer. However, it is a car built out of compromise, as indeed it has to be. We hope to show you how it can be tailored to suit your personal needs and tastes. Let's start by taking a look at the engine.

Chapter 3

Engines

VR6 conversions can look very sanitary—who would believe this is anything other than a factory installation? HPA Motorsports' VR6 New Beetle is a perfect example of how things should look. *Dean Kirsten*

The New Beetle, despite its retro styling, which so clearly echoes that of its air-cooled predecessor, is, under the skin, a thoroughly modern car in every way. The original Beetle was rear-engined and air-cooled, while the New Beetle is, of course, front-engined and water-cooled, sharing its drivetrain with the fourth generation VW Golf. As with the Golf 4, both gasoline and diesel engines are available to New Beetle owners.

One of the biggest problems faced by people wishing to modify the engine of their New Beetle is the inescapable fact that Volkswagen has done a fine job of engineering! In today's environmentally sensitive world, motor manufacturers spend literally millions in their quest to design engines that produce the minimum of emissions, yet offer optimum performance in return for modest fuel consumption. This drive for efficiency makes it difficult for the aftermarket industry to come up with new ways to boost power output without infringing on strict emission laws. Long gone are the times when you could buy a new car and then install whatever exhaust or induction system that happened to please you. The days of the blown big block are numbered.

However, human nature being what it is, despite the imposition of ever more stringent emissions limitations, there will always be those who seek out the loopholes in legislation that allow them to make the most of a difficult situation. It is a case of supply and demand—the New Beetle owner demands performance upgrades from the aftermarket, a demand that the aftermarket is striving to supply!

However, before we take a look at what the performance industry has to offer, we need to cast our eyes back over the last quarter-century to trace the bloodline that leads us today to the power behind the New Beetle. The lineage of the Golf 4's gasoline engine, and hence that of the New Beetle, can be traced to the 1.5-liter four-cylinder inline unit first used in the original Golf (Rabbit), way back in 1974. It began life as a relatively unsophisticated design, with a non-cross-flow aluminum cylinder head, cast-iron engine block, and a single overhead camshaft opening the valves via a "shim and bucket" system. These engines were incredibly reliable and soon proved to be very receptive to performance tuning. As if proof of this was needed, in 1976 in Europe, Volkswagen launched its legendary 1.6-liter Golf GTi, the first of what have become known as the "hot hatchbacks," in deference to the body style.

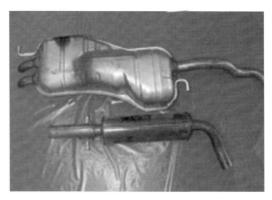

The stock exhaust system is efficient in terms of noise reduction but restricts power output. Changing this system should be high on your list of priorities. *New Dimensions*

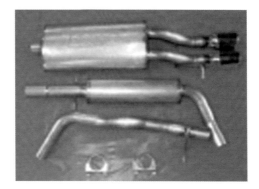

Borla exhaust is typical of the higher-quality systems on the market. It is manufactured from T-304 aircraft-quality stainless steel and should last a lifetime. It is a "cat-back" system, meaning that it installs downstream of the factory catalytic converter. *New Dimensions*

Installation of some aftermarket exhaust systems can require splicing into the original system. Most, however, are straight bolt-on replacements. *New Dimensions*

Some designs of exhaust system necessitate making a small cutaway in the rear apron. This looks more sporting but may not appeal to the owner who wishes to return his car to stock at a later date. Others, like this Neuspeed system, feature these trick-looking exhaust tips. Their large bore and upswept design are reminiscent of European DTM systems. *Neuspeed*

The basic fuel-injected 1.6-liter engine of the GTi grew in size to 1.8 liters in 1982, thanks to an increase in both bore and stroke—81.0mmx86.4mm instead of 79.5mmx80.0mm—which resulted in a small increase in both power (112 horsepower, up from 110 horsepower) and torque (109 ft-lb, up from 101 ft-lb). While these may appear to be insignificant increases, what made the 1.8-liter engine so much better than its predecessor was the way in which it delivered its performance. Maximum power was now produced 300 rpm lower down the rev range while torque—the more significant factor in a fast road car—reached its peak some 1,300 rpm earlier. This had the effect of making the car feel less "busy" when pushed hard.

The same basic engine was also used in other Volkswagen products, such as the Passat, Quantum in the United States, and Audi 80, in which its capacity was increased to 2 liters. This increase in size gave tuners a simple means of uprating the early Golf by making use of the bottom end of the

Borla tailpipes, with their polished "intercooler" tips, are very attractive. They clear the rear apron without trimming. *New Dimensions*

Passat engine in association with the more efficient top end (i.e., cylinder head and induction) of the contemporary Golf GTi.

Volkswagen also offered a 16-valve version of the basic 1.8-liter engine in 1985, although this was not available in the U.S. market until the 1986 model year in the Scirocco, and the 1987 model year in the Golf and Jetta. The European-specification 16-valve engine produced 139 horsepower at 6,100 rpm and 124 ft-lb of torque at 4,250 rpm. The American version had to make do with only 123 horsepower at 5,800 rpm, because it was tuned for more low-rpm torque to better suit the American driving style and the lower speed limits.

On paper, at least, these 16-valve engines looked to offer significantly more performance than the original 8-valve motors but, in reality, there was little choice between them. While the 16-valve-engined car was certainly quicker at the top end of the rev range, it felt sluggish in comparison to the 8-valve model at lower engine speeds. Both cars had their fans—but it is the original 8-valve model that people tend to regard with the most affection.

When the New Beetle was launched, it was offered with a choice of either 2-liter gasoline or 1.9-liter TDI (Turbo Diesel Injection) engines. Although they are similar in many respects to the earlier units, including previous diesel engines, they differ in many vital areas. One such variation is that the new gasoline engines have been designed in such a way that there is no longer any need for a separate intermediate shaft to drive the oil pump and distributor, thereby reducing weight and frictional losses. A new high-volume oil pump is driven off the crankshaft by way of a chain drive, while the ignition system is now a static high-voltage design that does not require a distributor as such.

We shall look in detail at the basic 2-liter gasoline and 1.9 TDI engines to show to what lengths Volkswagen has gone to improve them over the engines of the old Golf 3 and Jetta 3.

The engine block of the gasoline engine (factory code AQY), although superficially similar to the one used previously in the Golf 3 and Jetta 3 models, is in fact shorter by some 18 millimeters, and the connecting rods have also been reduced in length by a similar amount. The aim of this is to reduce the overall height of the engine, thereby allowing a lower hood (bonnet) line. In addition, the angle of the engine in relation to the body is changed slightly, necessitating the use of a redesigned oil pan (sump), which is now cast in aluminum for lighter weight and greater rigidity.

There are further differences between the new engines and most versions of the old A3-style engine used in most markets. Although the more

Zender's project car shows how the choice of exhaust system can alter the style of the car. Twin-pipe design looks very purposeful. *New Dimensions*

More conventional dual rolled tip exhaust gives a much sportier look to the rear of the New Beetle, implying power. This is another style that does require modifying the rear apron. *New Dimensions*

How about this Zender design? It looks just like the "zoom tube" tailpipe you used to be able to buy to fit your old air-cooled Bug. Perfect for the "retro" look! *New Dimensions*

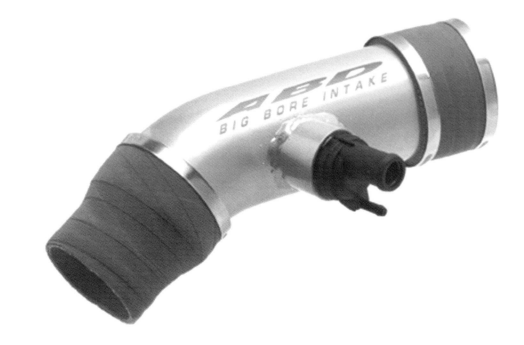

Autobahn Designs (ABD) was among the first to offer replacement inlet systems for the New Beetle. The big-bore inlet pipe helps to increase airflow and therefore boost power output. *Autobahn Designs*

ABD also offers a complete replacement air-filter system, based around a K&N filter. The red anodized bracket adds a welcome dash of color to the engine bay. *Autobahn Designs*

stringent emissions regulations of the U.S. market forced this change to be adopted with the introduction of the A3 models, they were new to the rest of the world with the A4 chassis cars. The new engines have a completely new cylinder head utilizing a cross-flow design (i.e., the inlet and exhaust ports are on opposite sides of the engine). The inlet manifold is a long, curved component, which passes over the top of the cylinder head, providing long airflow to help with bottom-end (low rpm) torque. The manifold is also intended, says Volkswagen, to offer a degree of crash protection in the event of a front-end impact, although this is a feature that few New Beetle owners will wish to put to the test!

Looking at the AQY engine as a whole, we find that it has a gray cast-iron block and eight-valve aluminum cylinder head with 40-millimeter inlet and 33-millimeter diameter exhaust valves operated by 35-millimeter diameter hydraulic bucket tappets. Valve lift is a moderate 10.5 millimeter (0.413 inch) for both inlet and exhaust valves. Each of the four cylinders is equipped with its own individual fuel injector, which is designed to allow air to mix with the incoming fuel for better atomization. This design is known as an "air-shrouded injector," the benefits of which include better low-speed running and improved combustion, and hence reduced emissions.

Neuspeed P-Flow air-filter system eliminates the restrictive factory air box and allows a more direct flow of air into the MAF meter in the intake system. This results in a boost in power output of as much as 8 horsepower. *Neuspeed*

Considerable development work has been done to reduce frictional losses and weight. This can clearly be seen when one takes a look at the pistons of the AQY-series engines. First of all, the skirt (or wall) of each piston has been coated with graphite to reduce friction against the cylinder walls, while the wrist (gudgeon) pins are kept as short as possible to reduce weight. Furthermore, to help lower the temperature of the piston crown, oil is sprayed on the underside of each piston by a spray nozzle located at the base of each cylinder.

In common with virtually every modern engine, the New Beetle relies on what is termed an ECU (Engine Control Unit) to monitor and control all functions relating to the fuel and ignition systems. In the case of the New Beetle's AQY-series engine, the ECU used by the Motronic 5.9.2 engine management system gathers information on the position of the camshaft to accurately determine the ignition settings. The camshaft gear incorporates a measuring wheel with two cutouts that pass in front of a Hall sender. With every 90 degrees rotation of the crankshaft, the Hall sender sends a signal to the ECU, the benefit of this being that all the information necessary to fire the engine from cold can be gathered within half a turn of the crank.

Information relating to the composition of the exhaust gases is gathered at two points in the

New Dimensions installed one of Neuspeed's P-Flow intake systems on its project "Purple HaZe" New Beetle with great results. *New Dimensions*

exhaust system by means of a pair of Lamda probes. One is situated in the exhaust manifold, at the point where the four primary exhaust pipes merge into two, the other being downstream of the catalytic converter. As a catalytic converter must reach its optimum operating temperature to be fully effective, there is a secondary air system (official name: Secondary Air Injection Valve) incorporated

Neuspeed's P-Chip, claimed to be the most advanced replacement ECU chip on the market, has been developed specifically for use on U.S.-specification vehicles. Increased power out put (as much as 13 horsepower) and improved torque are just two advantages of the P-Chip. *Neuspeed*

The impressive factory 1.8 Turbo gasoline engine is viewed by most within the industry as just a springboard to greater things. The KKK K04 turbo replaces the original K03 unit for an impressive power gain. *Autobahn Designs*

into the engine design, whereby a pump introduces air into the area around the exhaust valves. This results in unburned gases being burned in the first stages of the exhaust system, reducing emissions.

In a further quest to keep the environment clean, vapors from the engine block, cylinder head, and sump are sucked out of the engine by a vacuum created in the inlet manifold. To prevent this vapor from freezing in cold weather conditions, the entry point into the manifold is preheated by a heating element.

The 2.0-liter New Beetle's engine bay is dominated by the induction system, with the cast aluminum inlet manifold sweeping up and over the engine. This manifold really represents the final stage in the passage of air into the engine via the Multipoint Fuel Injection, which forms part of the Motronic 5.9.2 engine management system (EMS) used on all gasoline-engined New Beetles. The heart of the EMS is the Mass Air Flow (MAF) sensor, which accurately monitors intake airflow, allowing precise control of the air/fuel mixture, helping to reduce emissions and improve fuel economy. Unlike most other MAF sensors, that of the New Beetle is encased in a glass membrane, which protects it from contaminants in the intake airflow. Other more conventional MAF sensors are traditionally susceptible to contamination from moisture and oil vapor.

Neuspeed's K04 turbo kit includes a set of Beru plugs, low-temperature (180°F) radiator thermostat, and matching fan switch. Specially ported exhaust manifold is optional. *Neuspeed*

The New Beetle's MAF sensor relies on information supplied by two sensors (most systems have just one), one monitoring airflow upstream of the intake heating element, the other downstream. The Engine Control Unit (ECU) takes the readings from both these sensors and uses them to calculate the mass airflow. The use of two sensors also allows the ECU to detect reverse airflow in the intake system, a consequence of complex airflow dynamics brought about by the opening and closing of the valves—conventional systems do not have this facility and are therefore unable to accurately regulate the intake system at all points in the operating range of the engine.

The New Beetle has what is called a "distributorless ignition," with two double-ended coils, which each supply voltage to two cylinders simultaneously. This is because the ignition operates a "waste spark" system. As the pistons in one pair of cylinders approach TDC (top dead center), the ECU tells the appropriate coil to send a spark to the corresponding spark plugs. Only one of the two cylinders is on the compression stroke, the other being on the exhaust stroke; therefore, despite two plugs firing at the same time, only one actually contributes to the combustion process. The other is "wasted," as the exhaust valve is open at the time of ignition.

If you expect to push your car hard, especially in hotter conditions such as those found in states like Arizona, an aftermarket oil-cooler is recommended to keep oil temperatures to a reasonable level. *New Dimensions*

The 150-horsepower 1.8 Turbo engine could be considered the ultimate development of the original 1.8-liter four-cylinder unit of old—but it is far more than a simple bolt-on aftermarket turbo installation! It features a unique 20-valve cylinder head (with 5 valves—3 inlet and 2 exhaust—for every cylinder) with dual overhead camshafts in the search for optimum volumetric efficiency. Forced induction is taken care of by a KKK K03

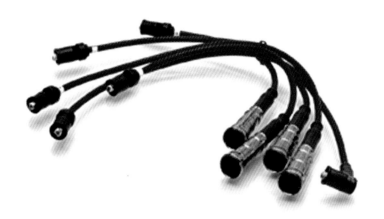

Stock factory plug leads are adequate for basic driving, but high-performance conversions can place a strain on the ignition system. The first step should be to install a set of aftermarket silicone leads, such as these from Autobahn Designs. *Autobahn Designs*

Neuspeed's 8-millimeter silicone leads feature solid copper cores for improved conductivity. Available in red or yellow, they help to brighten up the engine bay. *Neuspeed*

The 1.9 TDI engine in the New Beetle has been improved over its predecessors in a number of ways, including the use of a new intake manifold flap, an EGR (Exhaust Gas Recirculating) valve integrated with the manifold flap housing, higher fuel injector opening pressure, smaller fuel injector lines with nonreturn valves, and intake air silencer and a redesigned MAF sensor with reverse flow detection.

All diesel engines have a tendency to stop running when the throttle is shut, due to their very high compression ratio (19.5:1.) This can be felt by the engine wanting to "shudder" when slowing down. To prevent this, Volkswagen included an intake manifold flap that helps to reduce compression pressure when the throttle is closed, by preventing more air from entering the induction system. This flap is operated by a vacuum diaphragm actuated by a changeover valve, which is, in turn, controlled by the ECU.

To reduce emissions, improve fuel consumption, and cut down on engine noise, Volkswagen also changed the design of the fuel injection system used on the New Beetle's diesel engine. This now includes nonreturn valves in place of the former check valves used on the fuel distribution system, allowing excess fuel pressure to bleed off once each injector closes. To further reduce engine noise—especially the whistling developed by the turbocharger at engine speeds over 1,700 rpm—an air intake silencer is fitted which fine-tunes the sound waves generated by the induction system when the engine is under positive boost conditions.

The MAF sensor is similar to that used on the gasoline engine, except that it does not use an integrated air temperature (IAT) sensor. The new MAF sensor, with reverse-flow detection, relies on two sensors to measure intake airflow, mounted upstream and downstream of the intake heating element. As with the gasoline installation, the readings taken by these two sensors allow the ECU to factor out data from its mass airflow calculations.

To show what incredible attention to detail Volkswagen pays to the control of emissions and optimizing fuel economy, the fuel system of TDI New Beetles with automatic transmissions varies from that fitted to those with manual gearboxes. For example, the fuel injection pump's output pressure has been increased from 850 bar to 950 bar (that's from 12,325 psi to 13,775 psi), while an inline fuel cooler has also been installed to reduce the temperature of the fuel, which is increased slightly due to the higher operating pressures. This pressure increase also necessitated a redesign of the fuel-injectors themselves, their opening pressure now being 220 bar (3,190 psi) rather than the usual 190 bar (2,755 psi). All this has been done in the quest for lower exhaust emissions.

turbocharger, feeding the engine via a grille-mounted intercooler to help reduce the inlet air temperature. The fuel injection system is a sequential multipoint design referred to as the ME 7.1 system. With its cast-iron cylinder block, forged five-bearing crankshaft, and aluminum cross-flow cylinder head, on paper, at least, the 1.8T engine does not seem especially sophisticated in comparison to other units offered by some of its rivals. However, the improvement in performance over the 2.0-liter gasoline New Beetle is dramatic, with a 0-to-60 time of just over 8 seconds, compared with the 2-liter model's more pedestrian 10 seconds. A top speed of over 120 miles per hour also proves there is plenty of hidden potential in the New Beetle.

Making the Best Even Better

In North America, many people ignore the possibilities offered by the TDI engine, even though it is regarded as being the best in its field. As Dave Anderson, managing director of Autobahn Designs (ABD) in Riverside, California, says, "There is a whole different type of customer who buys the TDI—they have a different mindset to everyone else. For my part, I never even thought about the TDI when I was looking to buy a New Beetle because of old prejudices, but they sure are different to the old-style diesels! They're smooth, have a ton of torque, and even sound good. You throw everything you thought about the old 'tractor diesel' out the window. These are good cars!"

ABD suggests the TDI customer begins by adding a free-flowing exhaust and an open air-filter setup, and rechipping the ECU. ABD works with Frank Wetterauer (of Wetterauer America, Inc., in Valparaiso, Indiana) on all its ECU development and has seen up to 130 horsepower (as opposed to the 90 horsepower stock output) with such modifications. The ECU upgrade is responsible for the greater part of this increase, offering greater horsepower with little effect on economy or tractability (pulling power and smoothness). With this kind of increase, the effect can be amazing. As Dave Anderson says, "You can drive it up in the mountains and the car just keeps going, yet you'll still get 45 miles per gallon or more. It's incredible."

Tim Hildebrand at New Dimensions, Santa Clara, California, agrees there is a lot that can be done to the New Beetle TDI, with even a simple exhaust system change (a Borla "cat-back" system being the preferred choice) used in conjunction with a K&N or P-Flow (by Neuspeed) intake kit, resulting in a useful five to six horsepower gain. Now that may not seem like a great deal but, in this day and age, gaining extra horsepower from an engine is not the easy thing it used to be in the past. Today's engines are so efficient straight from the factory that you have to fight for each and every spare horsepower!

However, by adding a New Dimensions "Power Box," the TDI owner can really start to wake up his New Beetle, according to Tim Hildebrand. It's proved ideal for people who are not looking to modify the original ECU unit and wish to keep their factory warranties intact. The black box simply plugs into the ECU wiring harness and can easily be removed at any time. You can expect to see a very useful 20 percent increase in power (up to 20 horsepower over stock), 30 percent increase in torque, and even up to 15 percent improvement in fuel economy. A perfect case of having your cake and eating it, too! The only drawback is that, to extract the best from the installation, the car needs to be set up on a rolling-road dynamometer after installation—but that's a small price to pay for such improvements.

Most people agree that the models most likely to come under serious scrutiny from performance enthusiasts are the 2-liter gasoline and 1.8-liter turbo New Beetles. No disrespect to the 1.9 TDI, but it seems the world isn't quite ready for race-ready diesels—yet! All that is sure to change in the future, though, as gas prices continue to rise throughout the western world. In the meantime, however, greatest industry interest has been focused on the two gasoline-fueled models—and there have already been some pretty exciting developments in the comparatively short life of the New Beetle.

In the words of Dave Anderson of ABD, the 2-liter is "a little anemic—at least, that was our first impression. We were lucky as we got one of the early cars, but it just wasn't very exciting. It was a smooth car and around town it was a pleasure to drive. As a grocery-getter, it was great, but if someone wanted something to haul ass, then this just wasn't it." The problem is that, at around 2,800 pounds (roughly 1,300 kilograms), the New Beetle is no lightweight. The gasoline engine is a fine motor but its potential is slowed by the extra weight it has to drag around. When the original Mk1 Golf GTi was launched in 1976, it came with 110 horsepower, 5 down on the New Beetle, but the whole car weighed almost 1,000 pounds less! No wonder that first GTi won so much admiration for its get up and go—the New Beetle, by comparison, feels ponderous and lacking in real zip.

Dave's recommendations for the 2-liter New Beetle follow a tried and tested format, with intake and exhaust upgrades being the first on the list, followed by ECU reprogramming, and maybe a camshaft change. New Dimensions concurs, offering four stages of tuning for the 2-liter, starting with a basic Neuspeed P-Chip (replacement ECU program) and either a K&N or Neuspeed P-Flow air-filter swap. With this the New Beetle owner might see something in the region of a four- to five-horsepower gain but a greater sense of flexibility throughout the rpm range. Neuspeed claims its P-Chip is the most advanced computer ECU chip available, promising a precise ignition advance curve and fuel metering, resulting in smooth drivability throughout the entire rpm range. While some P-Chip installations can be carried out by the owner, the New Beetle is one vehicle on which the installation must be performed by the supplier.

Autotech's Q-Chip promises similar improvements, guaranteeing razor-sharp throttle response, improved acceleration, and improved power output without sacrificing drivability or reliability. P or Q—the choice of chips is yours!

The next step would be to add a "cat-back" exhaust system—current emissions laws in most countries don't allow you to modify the exhaust

Certainly the most visually exciting conversion is the Eaton supercharger installation, marketed by New Dimensions. This belt-driven blower guarantees a real "kick in the back," boosting power output by 50 horsepower and torque by a massive 46 percent! *New Dimensions*

system to bypass the catalytic converter or otherwise do anything that may increase exhaust emissions. To honor this legal requirement, many companies offer what are known as "cat-back" systems. As the name suggests, these are replacement exhaust systems that start right at the catalytic converter, leaving the front section of the system untouched.

There are several companies, such as Autotech, Remus, Borla, Supersprint, Neuspeed, and Techtonics Tuning, that manufacture exhaust systems for the New Beetle. Some basic systems are made from mild steel, but the majority of high-quality systems are made of T-304 stainless steel for long life. Each manufacturer offers a choice of muffler design, with one or two tailpipes, and Remus even offers carbon-fiber tailpipes on some of its systems. All offer exhausts that can be fitted without modifying the rear apron—some tailpipe arrangements, however, do require the apron to be clearanced, especially those systems that give the European "DTM" look, with upswept tailpipes.

New Dimensions believes that by adding a cat-back system, such as one from Borla, to a New Beetle already equipped with a replacement air filter and P-Chip, you should see an increase in power of anything

between 10 and 15 horsepower. Now that is starting to represent a seriously useful increase in power—around 10 percent—something any driver would be able to feel as soon as he nailed the gas pedal.

Each of the above-recommended conversions can be installed without the need to delve anywhere inside the engine, making them ideal for owners who wish to easily return their car to factory specification should they wish to sell it at a later date. However, to extract significantly more power, the next recommended upgrade is to install a replacement camshaft. Neuspeed offers a Sport cam which is generally accepted as being one of the best all-round cams available specifically for the New Beetle. It has an advertised duration of 256 degrees and a lift of 0.429 inch. Installing this cam with a cat-back exhaust, P-Chip and air-filter system should net an increase of around 15–19 horsepower.

Neuspeed isn't the only company, of course, to offer cams for the New Beetle (and Golf 4) range. ABD lists two Shrick cams for the New Beetle 2-liter gasoline engine, one with 268 degrees duration, the other with 272 degrees. Generally, the greater the duration, the higher the potential power output, but bear in mind this is usually at the

Neuspeed's Sport cam has an advertised duration of 256 degrees and a lift of 0.429 inch. Installing this cam with a cat-back exhaust, P-Chip, and air-filter system should net an increase of 15 to 19 horsepower.

expense of flexibility and low-speed torque. HÖR also has two cams for use in the New Beetle, sold under the Technologie Sport Hydro banner. The first offers duration of 260 degrees with lift of 0.421 inch, the other duration of 270 degrees and lift of 0.449 inch. Bear in mind, when considering changing the camshaft in your engine, that you should budget for a replacement set of cam followers at the same time, along with replacement valve cover gaskets and seals.

What can probably be considered the ultimate power upgrade for a 2-liter New Beetle, short of shoehorning another engine in place, is the supercharger conversion offered by New Dimensions. This centers around an Eaton M45 supercharger, similar to those fitted by Mercedes, Aston Martin, and Jaguar on their high-performance models. Forget comparisons with the old GMC truck blowers favored by the drag racers. The Eaton unit is compact and highly efficient, and it lends itself well to use on the New Beetle, where underhood space is at a premium. It is also a self-contained unit that doesn't rely on the engine's oil system for lubrication.

Installation of the Eaton blower is reckoned to take around four hours. Fitting is made easier by the fact that the New Dimensions kit comes complete with all necessary equipment to make installation on the New Beetle a snip. A machined aluminum support and drive system, throttle body support, intake pipe, and manifold adapter all form part of the ND kit, resulting in a factory-looking conversion.

New Dimensions is justifiably proud of the conversion, stating: "The Eaton supercharger provides improved horsepower and torque, at lower engine rpm, by pumping extra air into the engine in direct relationship to crankshaft speed. The positive connection yields instant response, in contrast to turbochargers, which must overcome inertia and spin-up speed as the flow of exhaust gas increases. The supercharger is a way to get around 'turbo lag.'"

So what can a New Beetle owner expect for his investment in terms of performance gains? On ND's own demonstration vehicle, the Eaton supercharger installation is complemented by a 2.25-inch Borla cat-back exhaust system and, even with a modest 7-psi boost, the estimated power output is in the region of 165 horsepower at 5,500 rpm—some 50 horsepower more than stock.

However, the greatest plus is the increase in torque at low rpm: ND reports a massive 46 percent increase in torque at 2,000 rpm, from 81 ft-lb (stock) to a very useful 142 ft-lb. Dyno tests have shown as much as 189 ft-lb at 3,000 rpm! As European Car magazine reported, "That's a difference you can feel!"

The ultimate production New Beetle—until the advent of the mighty RSi model—is the turbocharged 1.8T which in factory trim produces some 150 horsepower at 5,800 rpm and 162 ft-lb of torque at between 2,200 and 4,200 rpm. Yes, you did read that right: The 1.8T has the flattest torque curve in history. It's torque that is of the most use out on the open road, as torque equals pulling power up the hills, when overtaking or when accelerating hard.

Whenever you carry out any major engine conversion, it is highly recommended that you book a dyno session with an experienced specialist. Here, a Golf cabriolet is put through its paces on Neuspeed's chassis dyno. *Neuspeed*

When the 1.8T was launched in the United States in June 1999, it was immediately welcomed with open arms, not only by the customer at the local dealership but also by the aftermarket industry. This was a New Beetle that really offered great possibilities. However, as Autotech says, the engine of the 1.8T has been so well developed that it feels that it is no longer possible to simply install an ECU chip and see massive percentage gains in power and torque. Dave Anderson of ABD says, "In stock form, the 1.8T feels a whole lot faster than the 2-liter. I am not a turbo fan," he confesses, "in fact, you're talking to the wrong guy about convincing everybody to buy a turbo, but the 1.8T is a whole lot faster—it'll reach 100 without thinking about it, where in the 2-liter you had to keep on the gas for a while."

As the same basic engine is fitted to the Golf 4 and Passat (and, indeed the Audi TT), it would be easy to assume that any ECU chip conversions for these cars would swap straight into the New Beetle 1.8T. Not so. As Dave Anderson says: "VW threw a monkey wrench into the works and gave us a new ECU, and the computer programs we knew from the Passat and Golf don't apply. The rules have changed! The smoothness that could be felt on the Passat and Golf 1.8T was not there on the New Beetle." Why the changes?

Different vehicle weights, gearing, perceived market—and hence the way the vehicle is expected to be driven—all affect the way in which the ECU is programmed at the factory. Well, nobody ever said that tuning a modern car was going to be easy! In fact, times are getting harder for the aftermarket industry, not only because of more demanding emissions regulations but because, simply put, the manufacturers are doing a damned fine job themselves of extracting the most from such relatively small engines.

But what about the ECU from an Audi TT? Same basic drivetrain, yet with 180 horsepower in stock form, with a 225-horsepower version for those who want to go seriously fast. "That was our next thing," says Anderson. "We said 'let's swap computers because the Audi's going fast,' but it was totally different!" Other companies such as Autotech and New Dimensions soon reached the same conclusion, so research was directed elsewhere. However, what can be an obstacle to some is a challenge to others, leading New Dimensions to offer four stages of tune for the 1.8T, following what has become a tried-and-tested course among modern water-cooled cars. Stage 1 is to install a P-Chip and K&N air-filter system, resulting in an impressive claimed 180–190 horsepower. The P-Chip extends the rpm range of the turbo motor and offers smoother throttle response, increasing turbo boost from about 6 psi (falling to 4 psi) to around 11 or 12 psi throughout the rpm range. It also helps to rid the 1.8T of its somewhat lifeless character at lower rpm. An increase of between 40 and 50 horsepower at the top end is enough to make the 1.8T really come alive. But it doesn't stop there.

A Stage 2 conversion adds a Borla cat-back exhaust that results in a useful 190 to 200 horsepower, putting the New Beetle firmly in Audi TT territory. But there's more. There is always going to be a school of thought that says, "If big is good, bigger is going to be better." While that may not always be the case, it is partly true when it comes to the turbocharger on the 1.8T. This is because the stock KKK K03 turbo cannot cope with trying to produce higher boost pressures without hurting power output or reliability. This problem isn't unique to the K03, as all turbos reach a certain point at which they are no longer efficient—the answer is to fit a larger turbine unit.

New Dimensions, and others such as Autotech and Neuspeed, offer a replacement KKK High-Output K04 turbocharger, as used in the Audi TT. When fitted in conjunction with a specially programmed P-Chip, it sees the power output soar to a massive 210–220 horsepower. It is recommended that a new radiator thermostat and lower-temperature cooling fan switch also be installed at the same time, to reduce engine operating temperatures. The K04 turbo is physically the same size as the original K03, which makes installation a relatively simple process. The principal difference is that the K04 has a larger compressor and turbine wheels to allow it to produce up to 15 psi with ease.

The top-of-the-range conversion from New Dimensions is a turbo system that was developed in Germany by TEC. Along with a modified ECU, the kit comprises a 60-millimeter cat-back exhaust system, special turbocharger, ported and polished inlet manifold, larger inlet tubes between the turbo and airbox, air trunking from the grille to the airbox, and a fuel-pressure regulator. The outcome is a sensational 235 horsepower and a torque output of some 268 ft-lb (365Nm) at between 2,800 and 4,000 rpm, more than enough to embarrass even a 225-horsepower Audi TT owner!

So what's the next option? You mean you want more? Well, the simplest way to add some serious horsepower at this stage is to add a touch of nitrous oxide, with kits available from a number of sources, including Nitrous Express and NOS. Effective though it is, nitrous can only really be considered as a way to ice the cake, so to speak, by boosting horsepower on demand for relatively short periods. As a fun way to turn your New Beetle into a tiger, nitrous oxide injection does have a lot going for it. Correctly installed and dialed in, it is possible to see horsepower gains of up to 150 horsepower without any other modifications to the engine. However, it has to be emphasized that nitrous cannot be used all the time—it is only intended for use at wide-open throttle at higher rpm. Correct installation is vital, for nitrous oxide works by releasing extra oxygen into the engine, thus boosting oxygen levels and allowing more fuel to be burned. If you get the setup wrong, you could see an overlean condition, resulting in serious engine damage.

Probably the ultimate way to transform your New Beetle is to perform an engine swap, shoe-horning in one of VW's legendary VR6 engines from the Golf or Corrado range. With a full 2.8 liters and close to 180hp in stock form, the VR6 is one of the greatest engines ever built: it's super-smooth, very torquey and, best of all, is readily available on the second-hand market. Installation into the New Beetle isn't exactly a weekend "do-it-yourself" job but it can be executed by a skilled mechanic with access to full workshop facilities. There are two schools of thought on the conversion, one being to retain the original 2-liter transmission, albeit modified, the other to use the matching VR6 transmission.

The former option is the one favored by Dr. Boltz in Hermosa Beach, California, whose demonstration model has been enlarged to 2.9 liters and equipped with Schrick cams and an aftermarket exhaust system. This is sufficient to see power outputs exceed 200 horsepower. Retaining the original transmission has the advantage of making the installation a little more straightforward but there is a problem in that the gear ratios are not really matched to the VR6 engine (although it is possible to get by without changing ratios).

If the idea of using the original transmission ratios does not appeal, then the solution is to swap the internal ratios from the VR6 transmission into the New Beetle casing. If you choose to retain the VR6's transmission, you will need to fabricate new rear mountings to allow the drivetrain to be installed in the New Beetle engine bay. This is the route taken by Momentum Motorsport of British Columbia, Canada, among others. Their VR6-engined demonstration vehicle was taken several stages further with the addition of a Garrett T3/T4 hybrid turbo system supplied by Turbonetics in Moorpark, California. To take things to even higher levels, it is still possible to add nitrous oxide injection to this kind of set-up, with power outputs of over 350 horsepower being achievable!

The one area which probably strikes terror into the hearts of most people idly considering such an engine transplant is the wiring. Where on earth do you even start? Long gone are the days when transplanting an engine meant you only needed to hook up a fuel line and a live feed to the ignition coil. Today's computer-managed engines are in a different league, with complex wiring looms dedicated to each particular application. The answer is to work through everything logically, preferably with a shop manual for the New Beetle in one hand and one for the donor engine in the other. By careful study of the wiring diagrams, it should be possible to identify the common links between the two electrical systems. Your patience will be rewarded the moment you fire up your VR6-engined New Beetle!

Quite probably the ultimate engine conversion is to install the VR6 drivetrain from a Golf or Jetta into your New Beetle. The 2.8-liter VR6 is a superb piece of engineering that punches out 180 horsepower in stock form, but can be bored out to over 3 liters to produce in excess of 200 horsepower with ease. *Volkswagen*

Chapter 4

Transmission

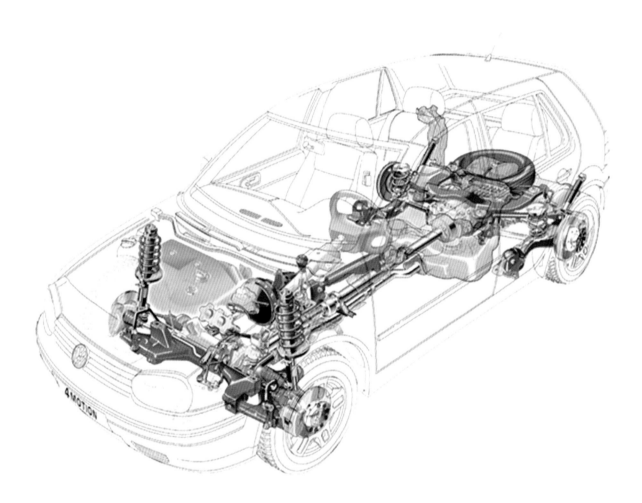

Volkswagen's Haldex four-wheel-drive system is used as part of the "4-Motion" package on the Golf 4. This system is used on the New Beetle RSi and will probably see use in other less exotic versions of the New Beetle. *Volkswagen*

Because it shares the same drivetrain as the Golf and Jetta Mk4s, the New Beetle is available with either a five-speed manual or four-speed fully automatic transmission. The manual gearbox carries the code number 02J and is derived from the former 02A family of transmissions used in the more powerful versions (VR6) of the previous models of the Golf and Jetta, while the automatic model is referred to as the 01M.

The manual unit is a cable-shift transmission, meaning that the link between the gear lever and the gearbox itself is by way of two heavy cables, rather than a series of mechanical linkages, as was the case in the earlier units used in the Golf and

Jetta. The advantage of the cable-shift design is that there are fewer moving parts to wear and fall out of adjustment, causing problems that can result in a sloppy gear-change.

The 02J is a fully synchronized transversely located gearbox with five forward speeds and one reverse. It is a well-proven unit that gives few problems if treated with respect and regularly maintained. The weakest link is the differential unit, which can shed the crown wheel (ring gear) if abused—the rivets holding the crown wheel become loose, allowing the gear to make contact with the transmission casing, with disastrous results. This has been a common weakness in front-wheel-drive

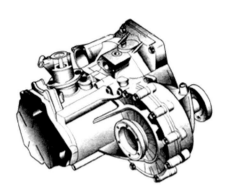

The 02J gearbox used in the New Beetle is a fully synchronized design with five forward speeds and one reverse. It is a well-proven unit that gives few problems if treated with respect and regularly maintained. *Volkswagen*

Volkswagen gearboxes for some while, and can be solved by bolting the crown wheel to the differential carrier. However, it should be said that this failure usually only comes about as a result of the owner making regular "drag race" starts, i.e., dropping the clutch at high rpm from rest. If this is the suspected cause of failure in your box, don't expect your dealer to carry out repairs under the factory warranty!

The 01M automatic transmission is the latest development of what the factory refers to as the AG4 series (as in four-speed automatic gearbox). Its full title is the AG4 Phase II Eta transmission, "Eta" being a Greek letter used to symbolize efficiency— and that's where the most development work has taken place, making this one of the most advanced automatic gearboxes in production. In an effort to reduce frictional losses, Volkswagen has incorporated new internal hardware, compared to the previous Phase II transmission, including low-friction bearings and a reduction in the number of clutch plates. The electronic transmission control module (TCM) has also been redesigned to take into account these upgrades and also to make the automatic gear changes even smoother.

Although the automatic gearbox option is a great choice for city driving, the manual transmission is of most interest to the driver seeking optimum performance. This situation might change if Volkswagen ever offers its celebrated "Tiptronic" gear-change system on the automatic New Beetle—a system that enables the driver to make swift gear changes by lightly tapping the shift lever forward to change up or pulling it back to change down. However, the Tiptronic option is currently only available on selected top-of-the-range VW and Audi models.

The first modification we would recommend for anyone with a manual transmission New Beetle is to install a so-called "short-shift" kit, the purpose of which is to reduce the throw of the gear lever between gear positions. Manufactured by Neuspeed,

the conversion (designed specifically for use with cable-shift boxes) reduces lever movement by approximately 40 percent and gives a more precise, sporty feel. The downside of this is that, under some circumstances, the gear shift can feel slightly "notchy" compared to stock. The conversion is very easy to carry out and can be completed by the average enthusiast using basic workshop tools and, in terms of value for money, it is hard to beat.

However, for those seeking the ultimate from their New Beetle, the best gearbox conversions are those manufactured by Quaife in England, and marketed in the United States by Autotech. Quaife is a family-run business of long-standing, with an enviable reputation for producing high-quality driveline components for a wide variety of cars. The most popular conversion Quaife offers for the New Beetle is the so-called Automatic Torque Biasing (ATB) differential, which can be considered a modern development of the traditional limited-slip differentials (LSDs) of old.

Quaife's ATB differential is designed to prevent the complete loss of drive that normally occurs when one of the driving wheels is on a slippery surface or is in a situation where it is lightly loaded— such as accelerating out of a corner. Most of us have experienced this at some time, especially in wet weather. As you put your foot down, the inside front wheel scrabbles for grip and forward motion is temporarily lost. Worse still, if you place one of the driving wheels in mud or on ice, that wheel will spin frantically. The ATB differential prevents this from happening—and here's how.

The Quaife differential is gear-operated, unlike the traditional LSDs, most of which contain a series of clutch plates that are prone to wear. Quaife describes the way its ATB operates thus: "Sets of floating helically cut gear pinions (see 1 in diagram) mesh to provide the normal speed differential action. To preload the gear packs, there

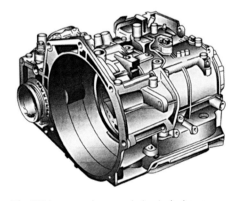

The 01M automatic transmission is the latest development of the AG4 series (as in 4-speed Automatic Gearbox). Its full title is the AG4 Phase II Eta transmission, "Eta" being a Greek letter used to symbolize efficiency. *Volkswagen*

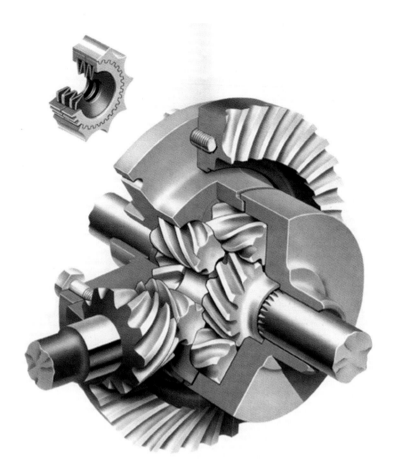

Quaife's ATB (Automatic Torque Biasing) differential prevents the traction loss that normally occurs when one of the driving wheels is on a slippery surface or when accelerating hard out of a corner. *Quaife Engineering*

is a selection of center spring discs available (see 2 in diagram). In the event of wheel slip, torque bias is generated by axial and radial thrusts (shown as red) of the pinions in their pockets (3). The resultant frictional force enables the driving road wheel and sun gear (4) to transmit a greater proportion of the torque. This effect is progressive, but at no stage does the differential lock solid—hence the inherent safety of the ATB differential." The principle behind Quaife's differential may not be the easiest to explain but, as experience gathered over many years of rallying and road racing has shown, the system works extremely well.

But don't think the ATB differential is a race-only component, for drivers of fast road cars can benefit, too. As anyone who has driven a high-powered front-wheel-drive car will be aware, such vehicles have a tendency to display what is known as "torque steer": The car will snake from one side to the other under hard acceleration. This phenomenon is caused by each front wheel losing its fight for grip on the road surface—and this is where Quaife's ATB differential can help, by automatically transferring torque from one wheel to the other as it is needed.

Quaife's differential units are not inexpensive, but they are virtually indestructible. (The author can vouch for this, as he has one installed in his own 200-plus horsepower rear-engined VW Beetle, which, despite using slick tires, has yet to suffer a

transmission failure on the drag strip.) The great thing about the ATB is that it is a direct swap for the original differential unit and does not require any special setting up process other than to follow the VW factory guidelines. Also it does not require the use of any special transmission oils, unlike some traditional LSD units.

The stock New Beetle transmission is a five-speed, fully synchromesh unit with a conventional "H-pattern" gear change. This is more than adequate for just about every application and will be the last thing that most owners will think about changing. However, those in search of ultimate performance from their modified New Beetle might like to consider one of Quaife's six-speed conversions, the most expensive of which features a race-style sequential gear change.

The idea behind converting to a six-speed gearbox is to enable the intermediate gear ratios to be closed up, and thus to allow the driver to make full use of the torque and power bands of the engine. A simple close-ratio five-speed conversion would mean that, if the stock top gear is retained, the intermediate ratios would be too tall for regular road use. And, if you install a lower top gear, you will run out of rpm when cruising on the freeway.

By fitting a six-speed conversion it is possible to retain a stock top gear and yet close up all the other ratios without affecting drivability. But the Quaife is more sophisticated than that, as each gear in the new transmission can run a numerically lower ratio in relation to engine speed. This means that the gear clusters will rotate more slowly, making the transmission more mechanically efficient and allowing it to transmit more torque.

The recommended conversion for use on the street is a fully synchromesh gear kit that is designed to be installed within the stock transmission casing with only minimal clearancing. The kit comes with all new ratios, mainshaft, and all other components needed to carry out the conversion. The ratios supplied with the kit are as follows:

1st	2.727:1
2nd	1.929:1
3rd	1.500:1
4th	1.200:1
5th	0.956:1
6th	0.800:1

In addition to this kit, there is a competition-only six-speed dog-engagement conversion which is similar to the above but does away with the synchromesh arrangement. The advantage of this is that gear changes can be made much quicker and without much consideration to niceties such as smoothness or silence. The disadvantages are that the kits are noisier and the gear changes have to be made in a very positive fashion, with downward changes requiring "double-declutching" to help synchronize gear speeds. The other feature of this particular conversion is that it is designed to enable fully clutchless gear changes—that's right: you simply select the next ratio without even having to depress the clutch pedal. This is possible by the use of interlocking "dogs" that mesh together as the driver selects a gear to provide drive. For anyone contemplating serious competition work in his New Beetle, this kit could be the answer.

We say "could" because there is an even better option for all-out race use, and that's Quaife's superb sequential six-speed dog-engagement transmission. Although intended solely for competition use, Quaife has proved, with its own Golf Mk3 demonstration vehicle, that such a conversion can be used on a road car as long as you don't mind the cost, gear whine, and noisy gear changes. It is a whole new gearbox unit that can be used in virtually any transverse front-engined car as long as there is a suitable bellhousing available. Being a bespoke, low-volume transmission unit does mean that the purchase price is very high— but what price perfection? A sequential gearbox means that the gear lever no longer has to be moved through the conventional H-configuration shift pattern, where selecting gears requires moving the lever back and forward and across the shift gate.

Instead, the gear lever in a sequential box only moves forward and back—pulling the lever back selects successively high gears, pushing it forward shifts down through the ratios. There are two obvious advantages to this, one being that changes can be made far faster, the other that there is a reduced risk of accidentally selecting the wrong ratio and possibly over-revving the engine.

To select neutral when at rest, the shifter is pushed right forward and a ring on the lever is raised. With the clutch pedal depressed, the lever is then moved forward into neutral. Selecting reverse means following the same procedure, except that the lever is then moved forward a second time.

On the road, the Quaife sequential six-speed gearbox is quite unlike any other. The clutch needs to be used to pull away from rest but, in theory at least, from then on there is no need to touch the clutch pedal again until the car comes to a complete halt. We say "in theory" because, in practice, clutchless gear changes are both noisy and embarrassing if you happen to have an audience. After all, the average onlooker is unlikely to know you have a custom transmission in your car and will, not unnaturally, assume that those brutally noisy gear changes are down to your inability to drive properly! Of course, you can make the changes considerably quieter by by using the clutch as normal, but even that won't do anything to stop the whine from the straight-cut gears.

Take your Quaife-equipped New Beetle out on the open road and you'll soon begin to think you have found an extra 50 horsepower under the hood, regardless of whether the engine has been modified or not. The lightning-fast gear changes and ultraclose gear ratios combine to turn your car into a rocketship as not only do you save considerable time on the gear change process, but it is possible to keep the engine "on the boil" from rest all the way up to maximum speed.

Although there are several gear ratios available to fit the Quaife box, the recommended choice in this case is as follows:

1st	2.615:1
2nd	1.937:1
3rd	1.611:1
4th	1.350:1
5th	1.160:1
6th	1.044:1

With a 4.467:1 final drive ratio, this equates to a drop of just over 2,000 rpm from first to second, 1,350 rpm from second to third, 1,300 rpm from third to fourth, just over 1,100 rpm from fourth to fifth, and only 800 rpm from fifth into sixth.

The Quaife sequential gearbox may not be the most practical conversion for the average enthusiast but, for those seeking the ultimate, there can be no substitute. All it takes is money. (And some ear plugs!)

Quaife manufactures a competition-only six-speed dog-engagement conversion that dispenses with the synchromesh arrangement. The advantage of this is that gear changes can be made faster, but without consideration for niceties such as smoothness or silence. *Quaife Engineering*

Chapter 5

Suspension, Brakes, Wheels, and Tires

Wheel and tire choice will always be a matter of personal taste. Be prepared to look around and check out several styles before committing yourself. OS Cup Racing wheels on ABD's project 1.8 Turbo look impressive—as do the big Brembo brakes they partly conceal. *Author*

There is no doubt about it, even in stock form, the New Beetle is a fine-handling car with excellent brakes, but there is considerable room for improvement. All mass-produced cars are built out of compromise—a balance between comfort, safety, and neutral handling—and the New Beetle is no exception. It comes with MacPherson-strut front suspension, first seen on a VW way back in the late 1960s—consisting of a combined spring and shock absorber that acts as the main suspension element. At the rear, there is a development of the well-proven compound torsion beam, used on the Golf and Scirocco models since the mid-1970s.

The front suspension is a development of that used on the Mk3 Golf/Jetta range, the principal differences being that the lower strut mounting is different and that there is no longer any way to adjust wheel camber (the angle of the wheel to the vertical when viewed from straight ahead) on individual wheels. Instead, it is now necessary to move the whole front suspension subframe from side to side to equalize the camber on each front wheel. There is 40 millimeters of caster offset built into the front suspension geometry to aid straightline stability. The design of the sway bar has also been changed—a modification which, as we shall see, can cause problems for people wishing to lower their New Beetles.

At the rear, the torsion-beam axle is a simple design, consisting of a single transverse beam with built-in trailing arms that support the rear hub and brake assemblies. The beam is designed to twist and act as a supplementary spring-cum-sway bar. Where the design differs from its predecessors is that the springs and shock absorbers are now totally separate units, allowing the shock absorbers to be mounted wider apart, so as not to intrude on trunk space and also to isolate the interior from excessive road noise.

All New Beetles are equipped with power-assisted steering and four-wheel servo-assisted disc brakes. At the rear, aluminum brake calipers are fitted, which help to reduce unsprung weight. Brake discs are ventilated at the front but solid at the rear.

The New Beetle features MacPherson-strut front suspension, which uses the combined shock absorber and spring unit as a main element in the suspension layout. Steering is by rack and pinion; front brakes are servo-assisted with vented rotors. *Volkswagen*

In common with the majority of modern front-wheel-drive cars, the New Beetle has what can best be described as very safe handling characteristics. When driven fast into a corner, there is little chance of spinning off into the undergrowth, as might be the case with a high-powered rear-wheel-drive car. This is because the New Beetle has a natural tendency to understeer—the front of the car will tend to run wide on a bend—as opposed to oversteer, in which the rear of the vehicle will want to step out of line.

Despite what Ralph Nader may have said about the old Chevrolet Corvair or VW's original Bug, there is nothing wrong with the latter situation as long as the driver is aware of what is happening. In fact, many sporting drivers prefer a car to oversteer as it allows them to set the car up for a high-speed corner. However, in the hands of an unskilled driver, oversteer can be harder to

correct than understeer and may result in a spin. If a driver enters a corner too fast with an understeering car, in most cases simply lifting off the throttle will bring the nose back into line. There are, however, limits—at too high a speed, lifting off the throttle can induce what is called "roll oversteer," a situation that could result in the rear of the car wanting to swap places with the front due to a sudden shift in center of gravity.

If the New Beetle has one fault, it is that its suspension is typically German—by that, we mean that it has relatively firm springs (giving what at first sight appears to be a stiff, sporting ride) but soft damping. This combination is fine for long spells on the freeway, but will mean that the car tends to wallow on long fast bends. The New Beetle also leans quite dramatically when pushed hard into a corner, despite the use of sway bars back and front.

Rear suspension uses Volkswagen's well-tried torsion-beam axle. Rear brakes are servo-assisted with solid discs, the calipers incorporating the emergency (hand) brake mechanism. *Volkswagen*

The simplest way to lower your New Beetle is to fit a set of aftermarket springs and retain the stock shock absorbers. Most specialists offer a range of springs; color-coding is used to differentiate between specifications. *Neuspeed*

A common misconception when uprating the suspension of a modern car is that simply installing stiffer springs will make the car handle better. After all, race cars have stiff suspension, so surely harder springs must make a positive difference. Well, no actually. Rarely does fitting heavier springs in isolation make a major improvement to the way the car handles—you need to look at the suspension system as a whole.

Fitting a set of lowering springs (i.e., shorter coils) can help to improve the handling by lowering the center of gravity, but the area that needs most thought is the damping.

Often people will fit very hard, lowered springs and then discover that the car rides like a truck, with a bouncy ride and increased road noise. They are then afraid to go a step further and install heavier shock absorbers (or dampers) because they fear this will make the ride even more uncomfortable. Not so—stiffer springs need firmer damping to help reduce the truck-like ride. The problem is one of extremes: Don't be tempted to fit the hardest springs and then the stiffest shocks you can get, unless you want to make your life a misery on the daily commute. A far better option is to take things one step at a time and listen to what the major suspension manufacturers (such as Koni, Eibach, H&R, Carrera, etc.) have to say. When

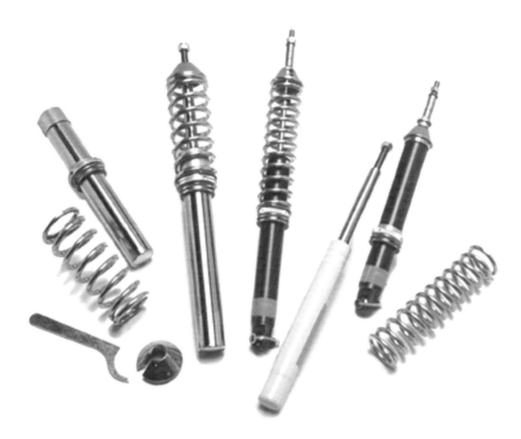

Autobahn Designs has worked closely with Carrera suspension products to develop a spring and shock absorber kit specifically for the New Beetle. This is a threaded-body design, which means that the ride height can be adjusted at the turn of a wrench. *Autobahn Designs*

they recommend a particular setup for road use, abide by their suggestions. Don't get drawn into the "hard is good, harder is better" way of thinking—your New Beetle won't love you for it. The same goes for aftermarket sway bars—stiffer is not necessarily better. Seek the advice of the manufacturer and err in the side of conservatism.

Most aftermarket specialists offer suspension packages, including sway bars, to suit just about every possible application. Neuspeed is one of the best-known manufacturers of performance sway bars and offers three designs: one front (25-millimeter diameter) and two rear (25-millimeter and 28-millimeter). The stiffer (i.e., thicker) rear bar is intended for sporting applications in which a tendency to oversteer is preferred. Neuspeed's sway bars are mandrel-bent, meaning that there is no distortion of the metal on the bends, and are formed from 6150 steel. The advantage of

this is that it does not need heat treating, a process that Neuspeed claims can distort the bar and leave an unsightly rough finish. The ends of the Neuspeed bars are machined to accept precision Heim joints, which allow accurate installation and adjustment, while each bar is powder coated for a long-lasting finish. Polyurethane bushes, which are supplied, ensure the sway bar is located more firmly than the stock rubber-bushed bar.

Fresh from the factory, the New Beetle relies on rubber bushes to locate the suspension. That's fine if you are after a soft, quiet ride, but if you want to sharpen up the handling of your car, a set of ABD's urethane suspension bushes is the way to go. *Autobahn Designs*

Even though the New Beetle's body shell is extremely rigid, there are still circumstances under which it will twist when the car is driven hard. Neuspeed offers a stress bar to tie together the lower front suspension pivots—a must for any car used in anger. *Neuspeed*

Several companies market upper stress bars, which bolt to the top suspension mountings to keep everything in alignment. This is Autobahn Designs' twin-tube stress bar fitted to the company's project New Beetle. *Autobahn Designs*

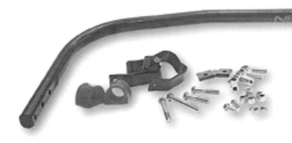

Although the New Beetle comes from the factory with front and rear sway bars, significant handling improvements can be made by the use of uprated aftermarket bars. Neuspeed markets bars for both front and rear of the New Beetle—this is a rear sway bar. *Neuspeed*

Of particular interest to the truly discerning owner are the hollow tubular sway bars offered by San Juan Capistrano–based Autotech. With technology borrowed from Formula One, Autotech's lightweight sway bars have a combined weight of just 18 pounds, yet are claimed to be as strong as conventional solid sway bars in roll stiffness. The advantage here is that there is less unsprung weight, resulting in more precise handling. Autotech's bars are available in 25-millimeter diameter for the front and 28-millimeter for the rear of the New Beetle.

One of the problems encountered when lowering a New Beetle equipped with the stock sway bars is that the driveshafts can make contact with the sway bar when the suspension is fully

Aftermarket rear sway bar shown installed on ABD's project car. *Autobahn Designs*

compressed. Aftermarket sway bars are designed to take this into consideration, by increasing the depth of the loop at the each end of the sway bar, where it passes over the driveshaft. If you do decide to retain the stock bars, you will know what that funny clonking sound is each time you go over a railroad track at speed.

With regard to spring and damper kits, several options are available. At the entry level, there are simple spring packages, such as VW's own TÜV-approved Accessory Sport Springs, which are manufactured in Germany by Eibach for Volkswagen. These lower the car slightly and firm up the suspension, but without upsetting the ride as we warned earlier. Other such kits are available from Neuspeed, H&R, Suspension Techniques, and Speedtech through outlets such as New Dimensions and Autobahn Designs. The amount they reduce the ride height varies between 10 and 30 millimeters, according to the manufacturers. Autotech lists HÖR Technologie progressive-rate spring kits for the New Beetle, which lower the car by around 30 millimeters.

Several leading companies offer shock absorber kits for the New Beetle, some complete with springs, others for use with stock or aftermarket lowered springs. Among the best-known is Koni, whose name has been at the forefront of suspension technology for decades. Koni offers fully adjustable sports gas shocks for the New Beetle. At the front, the damping rate can be adjusted by turning the knurled knob at the top of the strut from inside the engine bay, while at the back, the rate can be adjusted by first removing the shock and then turning the body in relation to the shaft (with the shock compressed). The ride-height

at the rear is also adjustable, thanks to a movable collar that locates the spring seat.

Bilstein, another well-known manufacturer of performance suspension products, lists two different shock absorber kits for the New Beetle, referred to as Heavy Duty (HD) or Sport. As the name suggests, the Sport kit is aimed at those seeking the ultimate in sports car handling, while the HD kit is for the person who drives his car every day, yet seeks superior handling to the stock application.

Neuspeed brake hoses are protected by a heat-shrink cover, which is color-coded according to application. VW hoses are coded red. *Neuspeed*

Neuspeed offers both drilled and slotted brake rotors for the New Beetle. These feature a black cadmium-plated finish to prevent corrosion (and to look good). *Neuspeed*

Koni also offers a coil-over suspension package for the New Beetle, which allows the ride height to be adjusted front and rear by the turn of a wrench. The lower spring mounts take the form of a pair of locking collars, which, when unlocked from one another, can simply be wound up or down the shock body with an open-end wrench. The advantage of this design is that it is possible to fine-tune the ride height of your car to suit your driving style and to take into account fender clearance when aftermarket wheels and tires are used.

Koni is not alone in offering such kits, for Autobahn Designs markets the Carrera "threaded-body" suspension kit, the rear shock of which features an aluminum body for reduced unsprung weight. H&R also lists a threaded-body coil-over suspension system for the New Beetle, which allows the suspension to be lowered by as much as 2 inches at the front and 3 inches at the rear. H&R also boasts lowering kits offering as much as a 5-inch reduction in ride height. Sachs also offers suspension kits for the New Beetle, which, with the springs supplied, reduce the ride height by approximately 1.5 inches.

New Dimensions offers three stages of suspension upgrading for the New Beetle, starting with simple replacement Neuspeed springs, in conjunction with shocks from either Koni or Bilstein. The next step up is the Stage 2 kit, which adds 25-millimeter front and either 25- or 28-millimeter rear Neuspeed sway bars. The final step is the Stage 3 package, which combines the sway bars with suspension kits from Koni, Sachs, Bilstein, or H&R.

ABD's Dave Anderson reports that many of his customers tend to follow this sequence: "Once you've replaced the original wheel and tire setup with different wheels and low-profile tires, you tend to get an unsightly gap between the tire and the fender. Many of our customers begin by purchasing new wheels and then come to us to find a way to get rid of that gap. Many start out by wanting to simply lower the car but, sooner or later, they come back wanting to upgrade the whole suspension. The next step up would be to fit a complete spring and damper package—we've had particularly good results from the Carrera kit—but we try to persuade them to install heavier sway bars at the same time. That way you end up with a complete, fully integrated suspension system, which really makes the New Beetle handle."

This is the front brake and suspension assembly on ABD's project New Beetle. Carrera suspension kit and drilled rotors are complemented by red calipers. *Author*

Rear of the same vehicle showing matching suspension and brake package. It certainly looks 100 percent better than stock. *Author*

New Beetle Cup race cars in Germany use 355-millimeter-diameter rotors with ATE-Racing calipers. If these babies don't stop you, nothing will! *Super GTI Magazine*

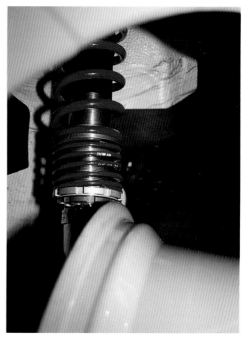

New Dimensions uses this impressive 330-millimeter rotor with AP four-piston caliper on its Purple HaZe project car. Three hundred thirty millimeters equates to 13 inches—that's big! *New Dimensions*

When selecting aftermarket wheels, there are several things to look out for before parting with your hard-earned cash. For example, check that there is sufficient clearance between the inside of the wheel and the suspension. *Author*

Big wheels and fat tires on a lowered car can lead to problems with fender clearance, especially on full lock when the suspension is compressed. Make sure your wheel supplier is prepared to stand by his recommendations before you purchase your new rims. *Super GTI Magazine*

Although the New Beetle body shell is considerably more rigid than that of most other sedans, largely thanks to the heavy roof pillars, there are still occasions when, pushed hard into a corner, the body shell will twist. If a car is to handle at its best, it is important to prevent this happening, and the simplest way is to install what is known as a strut brace, or stress bar. Many simply consist of a steel tube bolted between the top strut mountings at the front of the car. Others, like Neuspeed's and ABD's, feature twin tubes, which are less prone to deflection. Installation is straightforward and can be carried out by most home mechanics, as it requires only basic hand tools and a spare hour or two on a Sunday morning.

Autotech's stress bar is a single tube design in aluminum, but with a central adjuster for a precise fit in all applications. Autotech's bars also feature full-circle strut-top mounting plates for greater rigidity. It is not only the front end of the body shell that twists under load, for the rear end can also deflect when the car is pushed hard. To help prevent this, both Neuspeed and ABD offer rear stress bars to tie the upper shock mounts together. Although these bars do infringe on trunk space, they are a must if you are to extract the best from your New Beetle.

With your New Beetle now, hopefully, faster and capable of taking corners at far higher velocities than you ever imagined possible, isn't it time you

Although most people tend to think that "lower is better, " a car will often look its best when it isn't absolutely slammed. Try to set the ride height so that the tires sit centrally in the fenders. *Author*

started to think about how to make it stop? To be perfectly honest, you should really begin by upgrading the braking system before tackling any other area of the car. Human nature being what it is, however, all too often the brakes get left till last, largely because those fitted to most modern cars are already pretty efficient.

The brakes fitted to the New Beetle are 280-millimeter diameter vented rotors at the front, with 232-millimeter solid rotors at the rear. The fronts, being ventilated, are 22 millimeters thick while the solid rears are just 9 millimeters thick. The simplest upgrade is to replace the stock factory brake hoses with a set of aftermarket high-pressure braided-steel lines. Not only do these look far better than the originals, they also withstand high fluid pressures

far better and are, therefore, more resistant to "ballooning" when you push the brake pedal hard. New Dimensions offers its Carbonline brake hoses, which are Goodridge braided hosing encased within a carbon-look rubber coating for a different look and claimed excellent impact resistance.

The next step would be to replace the brake rotors themselves with either cross-drilled or slotted aftermarket products. The advantage of cross-drilled brake rotors is that they help to dissipate heat better than a solid or regular ventilated disc. They also perform better in the wet, as water is pushed into the holes. This is also the case with slotted rotors, but Neuspeed claims that this design helps to relieve high temperature gas build up between the pad and the rotor without weakening

Whenever you make any changes to the suspension, make sure you have the alignment checked. Failure to do so can lead to premature tire wear and poor handling. *Author*

the rotor in any way. Several companies offer drilled brake rotors, including ABD, New Dimensions, Autotech, and Neuspeed. New Dimensions offers its rotors as part of a kit, which includes a choice of either Mintex low-dust Redbox or Mintex C-Tech HPR brake pads. ABD also offers Metalmaster high-performance pads as part of its upgrade, while Neuspeed recommends FriTech (Friction Technology) Super Organic pads.

Simply replacing the lines and rotors on an otherwise stock braking system will by itself result in a considerable improvement in braking

efficiency, but it is possible to take things a couple of stages further. The first step would be to install a pair of 312-millimeter rotors from Audi's TT range. The kit, offered by Autotech and New Dimensions, among others, includes new hub carriers, rotors, pads, and calipers for a complete bolt-on, factory-style installation. This immediately transforms the braking of the New Beetle—the larger diameter of the TT's rotors means that there is greater leverage applied by the calipers, resulting in greatly improved stopping power. The components needed are as follows:

8N0 615 123	Left caliper
8N0 615 124	Right caliper
8N0 698 151	Pads (although it is better to use good aftermarket pads)
8N0 615 125	Carrier (two of these)
8L0 615 301	Rotor (two of these) (New Dimensions recommends having CNC-machined slots added for best performance)

Tim Hildebrand says, "The upright is the same as the Mk4. Some manufacturers plate the rotors, although I feel this contaminates the pad face and does not allow for proper bedding in. I would suggest powder coating only the exposed surface as an alternative, or machining/sanding off the plating prior to use."

Probably the ultimate brake upgrade can be found in the pages of New Dimensions' catalog: the 330-millimeter Race Brake kit. This visually impressive (and technologically superb) conversion is described as being "for those who demand extreme stopping power on the road and on the track." It consist of a pair of AP Racing cross-drilled 330-millimeter rotors with four-piston calipers and all necessary mounting hardware. Although primarily designed for competition use, the New Dimensions kit is fully TÜV-approved in Germany for street use.

Finally, we can't leave a section on handling without touching on the subject of wheels and tires. From the factory, all New Beetles come with 205/55x16 radials on 6.5J rims—either in aluminum or steel according to model specification. The first thing many owners want to do is to swap these for something a little larger—17- or 18-inch diameter wheels being the most popular choice. There are far too many wheels and tires on the market for us to make any recommendations on the design of wheel or choice of tire, but we will say that the most popular sizes are 18x8-inch wheels with 225/40x18 radials, or 17x8-inch with 225/40x17s.

You should note that, in the examples discussed here, the use of 18-inch wheels will result in a larger overall tire diameter. This would have the effect of not only raising the overall gearing of

Fitting low-profile tires to expensive rims requires skill and good equipment if damage is to be avoided. Don't always go for the cheapest deal in town—you only get what you pay for. *Author*

Fitting low-profile tires to expensive rims requires skill and good equipment if damage is to be avoided. Don't always go for the cheapest deal in town—you only get what you pay for. *Author*

the car but also making the speedometer under-read slightly. In itself, this is not a major problem but, if you so wish, it is possible to have the unit recalibrated by a specialist speedometer repair shop.

Yes, you can go bigger but you run the risk of having the tire foul either the fender or inner fender well when turning a corner, or even simply making contact with suspension components when at rest. Sometimes it really does pay to err on the side of caution when choosing your combination—unless, of course, you want to emulate the New Beetle RSi, which runs 18x9-inch rims with 235/40x18 tires. But then the RSi does have widened fenders.

But what are the main advantages of running larger-diameter wheels and low-profile tires? Well, to begin with, they look very cool. Okay, so that's not a very technical answer—or a good explanation to give your wife when you've just blown a substantial part of your household budget on some trick wheels and rubber-band tires. But it's an undeniable fact: The simplest way to alter the look of any car is to change its wheels. The major advantages of using larger-diameter wheels are that you can install bigger brakes without clearance problems and you can run lower-profile tires without upsetting the overall gearing of the car.

Tire profile, also called the "aspect ratio," is a measure of the ratio between the sidewall height and the width of the tread. The lower the profile, the shorter the tire for a given width—therefore, a 205/60 tire will be taller than a 205/55 (the "205" being a measure of the tread width, the "50" or "55" being the aspect ratio, expressed as a percentage of that width). Increasing the tire diameter as a result of fitting fatter tires on larger rims can—and almost certainly will—result in clearance problems but, by using lower-profile tires of the correct size, you can use bigger wheels and enjoy the benefits of wider tire tread without causing a headache.

Low-profile tires are a real aid to handling, too, for their inherently stiffer sidewalls mean less tire deflection when pushed hard into a corner, which in turn means more precise handling and better driver feedback. The downside of running ultra-low-profile tires (40-series and below) is that ride quality suffers, and you will almost certainly experience an increase in road noise transmitted to the interior. The cost is also considerably higher than other tires. But, as we said, they do look cool.

Once the tires have been fitted, have the rims dynamically balanced. Use self-adhesive weights and ask for them to be installed on the inside of the rim if possible. *Author*

Lowering the suspension of any car will, in most instances, help to improve its handling characteristics—and the New Beetle is no exception. There are several suspension kits available for the New Beetle which can be fitted at home by an enthusiast who has access to fairly basic tools and a few hours on his hands.

In this first photo series, we show you how we installed an H&R suspension kit to the front of a New Beetle. This work involved the removal of the original MacPherson strut assembly and its replacement with the new H&R unit. Remember, once you have carried out the installation, it is vital that you have the front end realigned at a specialist shop.

This view of the stock front suspension, showing the MacPherson strut layout, reveals that it is the same setup as used on the Golf and Jetta 4 models. That means products sold for the suspension of either of those cars will fit on the New Beetle as well. *Author*

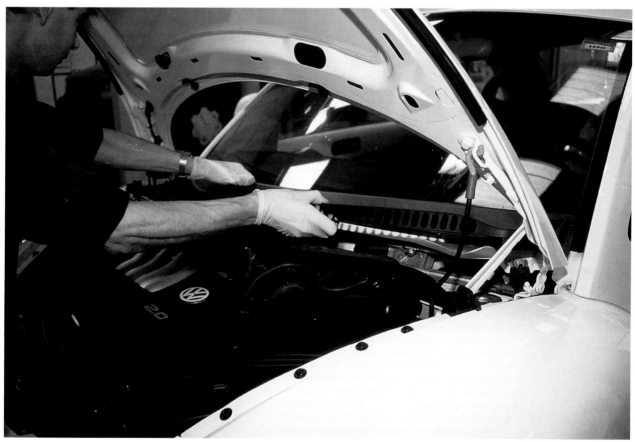

1. To gain access to the top suspension mountings, it is first necessary to remove the plastic rain shield from in front of the windshield. Be careful, as it can be brittle and can break easily. *Author*

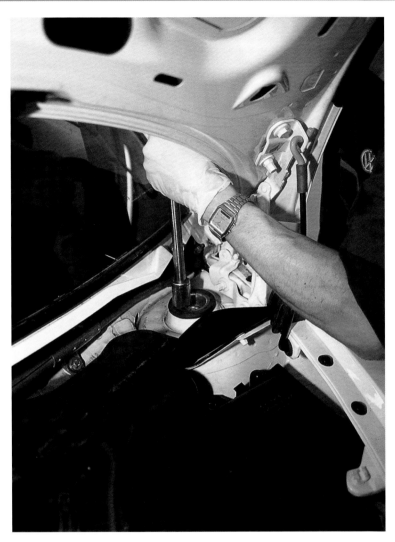

2. Top strut mounting needs to be loosened first of all. Use a socket and long extension bar to gain access to the nut. Don't lose any parts, as they will need to be reused later. *Author*

3. The bottom of the strut unit is located in the stub axle assembly by a pinch bolt. This must be completely removed. *Author*

4. Drawing shows detail of lower strut mounting. The correct way to remove the strut from the stub-axle is to use a factory tool, which is inserted into a slot and twisted to loosen the joint. A soft-faced hammer will work just as well. *Volkswagen*

5. Before removing the strut, you will need to unbolt the front sway bar mountings. Note the curve of the sway bar as it passes over the driveshaft. On a lowered car, the shaft can hit the sway bar when the suspension is compressed. *Author*

6. A few gentle blows with a soft-faced hammer should free the strut from the stub-axle assembly. *Author*

7. It may be necessary to undo the inner CV joint on the passenger side of the car to allow the driveshaft (arrowed) to move out of the way, so the suspension can be pulled down sufficiently to enable the strut to be removed. *New Dimensions*

8. With both top and bottom mountings now undone, the strut can be removed as a complete unit. Be careful, as it is quite heavy. *Author*

9. Now that the strut is out of the way, you can see more easily the pinch bolt system used to locate the lower end of the strut assembly. *Author*

10. Even when installing a complete suspension package, you still need to use the top suspension mounts. To remove these, you must compress the stock spring using a spring compressor. *Author*

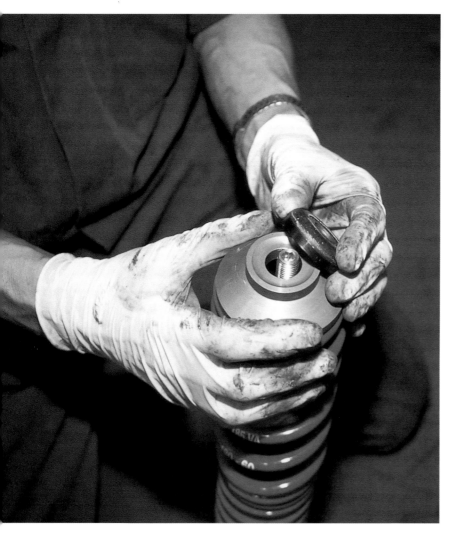

11. The large rubber bushing is reused (top right), as are the spacer and nut. The H&R strut is considerably shorter than the stock assembly. *Author*

12. The new strut needs to be assembled before it is fitted to the vehicle. *Author*

13. This is the stock strut assembly (right) compared with the H&R threaded-body kit (left). Note how much slimmer the H&R strut is in comparison to the original. *Author*

14. With the top of the new strut loosely installed, you can now engage the lower end in the stub-axle assembly. Make sure it is fully home, then reinsert the pinch bolt and tighten. *Author*

15. This is the completed strut assembly. The plated finish of the strut body and powder-coated springs looks great, compared with the original dull black units. *Author*

16. The great thing about a threaded-body suspension kit is that you can adjust the ride height at the turn of a wrench. The H&R kit allows the front end to be lowered 0.75–2.0 inches. *Author*

17. With the car on a flat surface, all that remains to be done is to check that the ride height is the same on both sides. *Author*

Now that we have lowered the front suspension of our New Beetle, it's time to turn our attention to the rear. Fortunately, this is a far simpler operation and will take considerably less time than is required to lower the front end. Once again we used an H&R kit, consisting of new shorter springs, adjustable mountings and uprated shock absorbers.

Note that installation of the suspension kit does not affect wheel alignment at the rear.

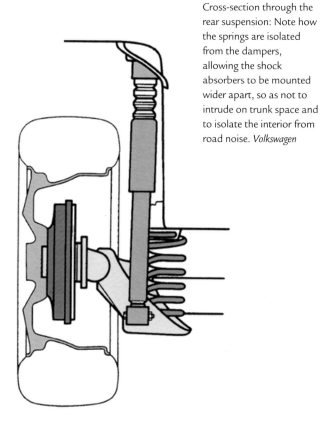

Cross-section through the rear suspension: Note how the springs are isolated from the dampers, allowing the shock absorbers to be mounted wider apart, so as not to intrude on trunk space and to isolate the interior from road noise. *Volkswagen*

1. This is what you see when you remove the rear wheel. The New Beetle's rear suspension assembly looks like a model of simplicity. *Author*

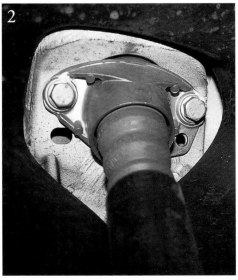

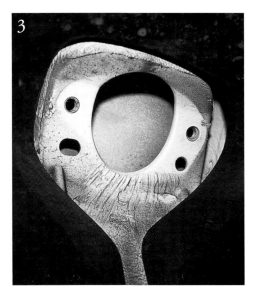

2. The top end of the damper unit is secured by two bolts, which are accessed from inside the fender well. It is easier to carry out this work if the car is placed on a proper hydraulic lift. *Author*

3. This is the top mount on the body shell. Clean away any accumulated dirt and grime while you have the opportunity. *Author*

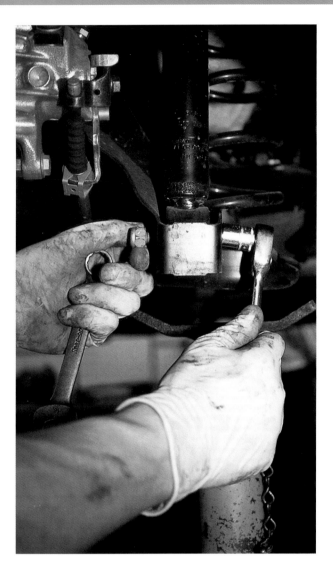

4. Remove the through-bolt that secures the bottom end of the damper to the torsion beam. You will need to support the beam while doing this. *Author*

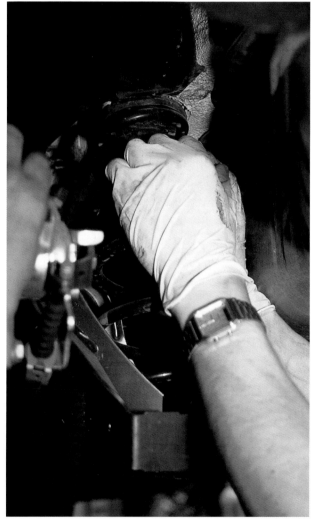

5. With the help of a friend, pull down the axle beam and remove the stock spring, along with its rubber bushes. *Author*

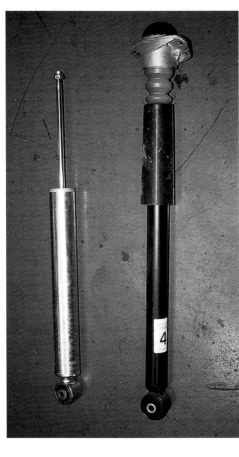

6. New H&R damper on the left looks compact alongside the original unit. *Author*

7. You will need to reuse the top mounting and bushes. Remove these by placing the old damper in a vise and using a pair of wrenches to remove the nut from the damper shaft. *Author*

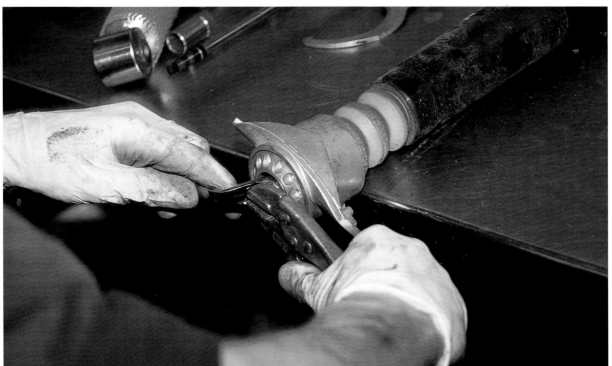

8. H&R kit comes with this trick billet-aluminum lower spring mount, which allows you to adjust the ride height at the twist of a wrench. *Author*

9. The lower mount is in three parts, two of which are screwed together on either side of the bottom spring mounting on the torsion beam. An open-end wrench is used to tighten the assembly. *Author*

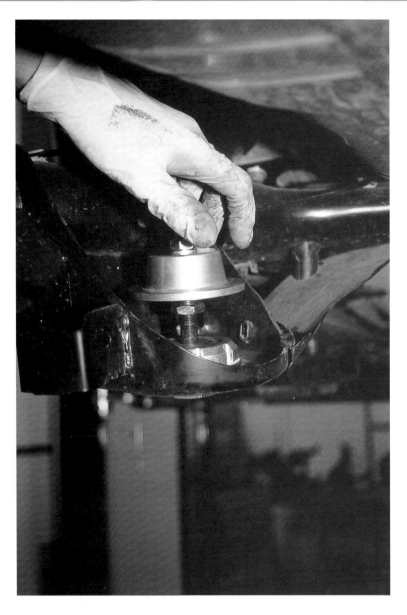

10. The adjustable spring seat screws into the bottom portion of the mount. Coat the threads with some copper grease to prevent corrosion, which may make it difficult to adjust at a later date. *Author*

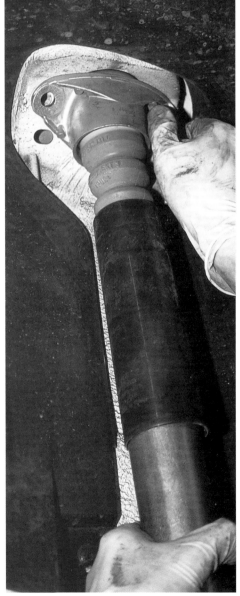

11. The damper needs to be assembled with the factory dust cover and top mount. This can then be installed on the car from below. *Author*

12. The factory rubber bush slips into the top of the new spring. If there is any sign of wear, replace with a new bush while you have the opportunity. *Author*

13. Pull the torsion beam down out of the way as far as possible and then install the new spring, top first. Note that the more tightly wound coil goes toward the top. *Author*

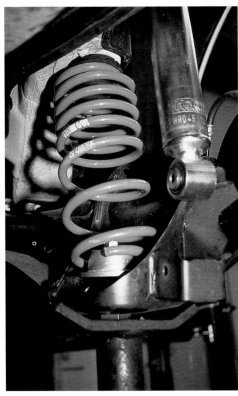

14. Locate the bottom of the spring over the lower mounting—supporting the torsion beam will help. *Author*

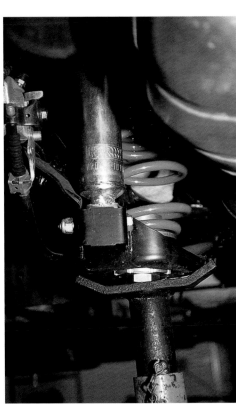

15. Place a jackstand under the torsion beam and gently lower the car. This will enable you to fit the bolt through the bottom of the damper assembly. *Author*

16. The completed installation. Ride height adjustments are made by rotating the lower spring mounting with an open-end wrench. Make sure the ride height is the same on both sides. *Author*

Chapter 6

Bodywork

Low, lean, and very mean—Bernt's V1 project car looks stunning in its tangerine pearl paint. Fenders are 1-1/2 inches wider than stock to accommodate fat aftermarket wheels. *Super GTI Magazine*

If you stopped virtually any owner and asked him or her what it was about the New Beetle which first caught their eye, the reply would almost certainly be "the styling." Few would cite the drivetrain technology or the safety features—or even how many miles per gallon the New Beetle gets on the freeway. Right from the very beginning, when the original Concept 1 styling exercise was no more than a rough sketch on a studio drawing board, the cute rounded body shape, so evocative of Volkswagen's original Beetle, was the most important element in the whole design.

Even though, when it was first exhibited, Concept 1 was destined to use the most up-to-date powerplant, anything from a high-tech diesel to a complex "zero-emission" hybrid engine, it was the body shape that attracted most attention. As production became more of a serious proposition, it was still the styling that created the most comment from the media, despite the decision to use the very latest drivetrain technology from the Golf and Jetta Mk4. It could almost have been powered by a rubber band for all some people cared—it was the styling that mattered. So why is

The New Beetle may have come into this world as a cute little pussycat, but even Volkswagen recognized its potential as a tiger. The New Beetle RSi has one of the most aggressive body kits imaginable. *Volkswagen*

The two-element rear wing used on the RSi gives a clear indication of the car's racing heritage. Its design has been heavily influenced by the appearance of the New Beetle Cup race cars. *Volkswagen*

One of the most aggressive looking body kits on the market is the V1 from Classics by Bernt. If you think the front end looks familiar, take a trip down to your local Ferrari dealer and have a look around. *Author*

The complete Bernt V1 body kit ready for installation. Note the special exhaust system used with this kit, which exits through the center of the rear apron. *Classics by Bernt*

it, then, that the first things the aftermarket industry began to develop especially for the New Beetle were body-styling kits? It came as no surprise that exhaust systems or suspension kits were on offer the moment the cars hit the dealerships, for many of these components had already been made available for the Golf and Jetta. However, one could be forgiven for thinking that new parts designed expressly to change (but not always to improve) the overall look of the New Beetle would be low on the list of priorities. Wasn't the car stylish enough already?

Well, in just the same way that some people like to add wings to Ferraris—or paint flowers on their VW Microbuses—there will always be those who want their car to look different from the one down the street. Not necessarily better, just different. That is strange thinking as, more often not, the reason people bought the New Beetle was because it already looks so different from any other car on the road!

The body shell of the New Beetle benefits from construction techniques that make it both immensely strong and very resistant to corrosion. In fact, despite being based on the same floorpan as the Golf and Jetta Mk4, the New Beetle is considerably more torsionally rigid than either of these two models. Special alloy steel is used for certain of the body panels, enabling them to be made thinner than usual to save weight. This steel is relatively soft when first formed and welded on the production line but attains its maximum strength when the body is passed through the paint-baking process, where temperatures reach approximately 170 degrees Celsius (338 degrees Fahrenheit).

This process means that the special thinner body panels end up being as strong as their thicker counterparts. Of course, as any owner who uses his New Beetle on a daily basis will quickly come to appreciate, not all body panels are made of steel—several, including the vulnerable front and rear bumpers and the fenders themselves, are molded from deformable plastic, called TPO (Thermoplastic Olefin). The advantages of this material are that it is resistant to careless parking damage, cannot corrode, and is cheaper to manufacture. However, as Volkswagen is keen to impress on its dealers, when refinishing these plastic panels it is necessary to use the correct materials, as use of incompatible paint products can lead to paint reactions and possible damage to the panel.

There are many simple bolt-ons that can help to transform the appearance of your New Beetle, some of which are intended to give the car a retro look, while others help to make this cute cuddly car look more aggressive. Kamei, the old-established German accessory manufacturer, markets a range of retro-styled products, including "stone guards" for the rear fenders, "eyebrows" for the headlights, and

door-handle "finger plates," all of which bring to mind the accessories the company made for the original Beetle back in the 1960s. In addition, there are bumper deco strips that bear more than a passing resemblance to the trim found on Deluxe versions of the old VW transporter.

Other manufacturers have been quick off the mark to add their touch of retro styling, among them Zender, the well-respected German aftermarket supplier. This company produces a rear apron that accepts its own sports muffler, reminiscent of the original "zoom tube" tailpipe, which proved to be a cheap and effective way to dress up the "pea-shooter" exhaust of an old Beetle.

This retro styling can be carried still further with the addition of a vintage-style roof rack from Parts Is Parts (PIP), which has proved to be a very popular (and, it has to be said, practical) accessory with owners of New Beetles. If that isn't your scene, then how about the rear luggage rack from New

V1 rear wing incorporates a third, high-level brake light, using the original brake light as a mounting point. This is ABD's 1.8 Turbo project New Beetle. *Author*

The V1 kit uses a central-exit exhaust system for an individual look, reminiscent of Porsche's Boxster. The mesh grille helps air to escape from under the apron. *Super GTI*

The hood of the V1 body kit incorporates two Ferrari-like vents that allow hot air to escape from the engine bay. Note the billet-aluminum detailing with Concept 1 logos! *Super GTI Magazine*

only possible problem area is color-matching if the panel has been supplied unpainted. But some companies offer an in-house refinishing service and are thus able to supply the wings ready to fit, painted to match your car.

Installation is very straightforward but requires a little patience if the end result is to live up to expectations. The most important thing to remember is to check and double-check before drilling holes. Some wings, such as the Cord or the Aerodymensions wing from New Dimensions, can be installed without drilling any holes at all, as they pick up on the mountings for the third, high-level, brake light. Fully DOT-approved, the Aero-dymensions wing features a Hella LED brake light in place of the original, which is no longer used. Other bolt-on body accessories that have proved popular are what have become known as "splitters"—small winglets that fit to the underside of the front spoiler, in the style of the European DTM-series race cars.

Splitters are relatively easy to fit and installation requires nothing more than basic hand tools. Most splitters pick up on the factory spoiler mounting points to facilitate alignment when fitting but it still pays to take your time and measure each side to ensure that yours are fitted symmetrically. Don't take it for granted that the factory mountings are exactly the same side for side, or that the aftermarket fittings are 100 percent accurate, as nothing will look worse than a car with a slightly lop-sided appearance.

One of the features of the original Beetle which endeared it to both the aftermarket industry and home enthusiast is the fact that the fenders are simply bolted in place. In fact, removing all the fenders of a Beetle required little more than a couple of wrenches and an hour or two of your time. Similarly, the New Beetle has fenders which bolt on, as do the front and rear aprons, meaning that it is relatively easy for these panels to be removed and replacement panels installed. This has made it possible for suppliers to offer complete body kits of fenders, apron, and side skirts, which can be installed without too much difficulty. Many companies even offer these kits ready-painted in factory colors to make the task even simpler.

Most of these kits are designed to make the New Beetle appear more aggressive than its soft retro styling suggests. Among the more stylish of these are the kits from New Dimensions and Classics by Bernt in Stanton, California. The New Dimensions kit, marketed under the Aero-dymensions brand name, includes front and rear aprons and a pair of side skirts. Manufactured from flexible polyurethane, the ND kit is designed to withstand a certain amount of contact with steep driveways—a common source of damage to spoilers and air dams molded from cheaper fiberglass.

Dimensions? Clearly reminiscent of the chromed racks fitted by many old Bug owners, the ND product is a stylish and fun way to improve the luggage-carrying capacity of the New Beetle.

There is a vast range of body kits for the New Beetle available on the aftermarket—something to suit virtually every taste and image. These kits range from the relatively mild to those verging on wild. Some kits consist of little more than a rear wing, front spoiler and, maybe, some modest side skirts. The more extravagant kits can include replacement fenders, hoods, front and rear aprons, wings, and side skirts.

Among the first aftermarket body panels to be offered for the New Beetle were simple rear wings to mount below the rear window on the tailgate. Designed to help improve the vehicle's stability at speed, these wings are easy to install and can be fitted by most home mechanics in a few hours. The

Projektzwo's show car is color coordinated from front to back. Fender extensions allow the use of wide wheels and tires for an aggressive look. The car is powered by a 3.2-liter VR6 motor. *Super GTI Magazine*

The rear of the Projektzwo kit looks very smooth. Note the rear apron with its wide cutout to accommodate a typical European wide license plate. *Super GTI Magazine*

Belgian RSD body kit is one of the most tasteful on the market. Wide fenders allow fitment of huge 19-inch rims without clearance problems. *Super GTI Magazine*

From the rear, the RSD kit shows off its unusual spoiler and central-exit exhaust system. Note the vents at the lower edge of the rear fenders. *Super GTI Magazine*

Retaining the original bumper panels, the ND kit incorporates the factory-installed back-up lights and front driving lights.

By far the most outrageous body kit on offer is the V1 styling kit from Classics by Bernt. This package is definitely not for the New Beetle owner who is shy and retiring! What makes the V1 kit so unique is that it includes complete replacement front and rear bumper panels, an aggressive rear wing, and, so as to accommodate larger wheels and tires, wider fenders for the front and rear. If that isn't enough, there is also a replacement hood, complete with air vents. The design of the front bumper (and the hood) is clearly inspired by contemporary Ferrari styling, with its 'smiling' front air intake and low-set driving lights. The rear bumper and apron panel are also uniquely styled, as they are designed to accommodate a custom exhaust system, marketed exclusively by Classics by Bernt. The system, which includes a small megaphone tailpipe, exits through the center of the rear apron, giving a whole new look to the rear of the car.

If there is one piece of advice I would offer to anyone considering changing the appearance of a

German specialist tuner, Dietrich, created this tough-looking body kit which features fenders widened by 1-1/2 inches. The kit is sold under the "XXL New Beetle Super Cup" banner. *Super GTI Magazine*

New Beetle, it is to sit down and plan your whole project before you start. It is very easy these days to go to your local VW accessory store and buy, for example, a set of wheels and tires for your car. But nothing else you ever buy will have quite such an influence on the way your New Beetle looks as a replacement set of "rims and rubber," so choose wisely. And bodywork—what was it that attracted you most about the New Beetle when it first appeared at your dealership? Was it the retro styling? Or did you look at the car as a whole and see it as a thoroughly modern design that begged to be turned into a slick-handling sportster? If it was the former, then perhaps it isn't such a wise idea to consider an aggressive body kit but, instead, to think more along the lines of those 'vintage-style' accessories, like the PIP roof rack or Kamei stoneguards. Certain colors suit the vintage look better, too, especially black or maybe red.

If, however, you prefer to walk on the wild side, then clearly the V1 or Aerodymensions body kits are for you. Perhaps you can add some race-style graphics, with broad stripes up and over the roof, similar to those of the Shelby race cars of the 1960s. Now that would spell "sports car"! If this is a little too avant-garde for you, then the next time you're

This rear wing from Kercher looks brutal. Its chunky design is very aggressive and "in your face"—perfect for the slammed street-racer-style New Beetle. *Super GTI Magazine*

Richard Straman in Huntington Beach, California (where else?), created this superb New Beetle cabriolet, complete with fully functional top and wind-down side windows. *Author*

sitting on the freeway, take a look at the cars around you—maybe there's a non-VW color that really appeals to you. Sure, Volkswagen came up with some very cool colors when it designed the New Beetle, but VW doesn't have the monopoly when it comes to neat paint hues. Giving your New Beetle a complete color change isn't a job for the faint-hearted but it will help to make your car unique.

However, by far the most radical redesign you can consider (for the time being, at least!) would be to create a cabriolet version of your New Beetle. Even though Karmann, the German coachbuilding company, has made no secret of its desire to build a New Beetle cabrio, the VW factory has remained tight-lipped about the possibility of a production version—and this is despite showing a Concept 1 cabrio at the Geneva motor show as far back as 1995. However, the design exercise looked so stunning, and captured so many people's imagination, surely it would only be a matter of time before somebody built their own New Beetle cabriolet—and that person was Richard Straman,

The sedan roof is cut just behind the windshield, with doors trimmed to match. Overall finish is to a very high standard. Will the long-awaited factory cabrio be as good? *Author*

The bra from Perfect Fit offers greater protection than most others on the market. A small opening in the bra shows off the original hood badge. *New Dimensions*

who runs a high-quality body shop in Huntington Beach, California.

The first prototype he produced was a nonfunctioning "roofless" conversion in Techno Blue metallic. However, that was only a taste of things to come, for a fully functional cabrio was under development. The conversion is far more than a matter of simply slicing the top off a New Beetle sedan and installing a folding top, for Straman strengthens the body shell by incorporating a substantial new subframe around the rear of the car and installing strengtheners through each rocker panel. The result is a body that is more rigid than the sedan from which it is derived.

The roof is cut off at the base of the rear pillars, the door pillars ("B-posts"), and across the roof behind the windshield. The door window frames are almost entirely removed, with only the front section adjacent to the windshield remaining to support the glass. The new rear subframe is then installed, along with cappings to finish off the top of the windshield, doors, and pillars. One of the most impressive features is the inclusion of electrically operated rear side windows The multilayer convertible top is complete with a full headlining and efficient rubber seals to ensure that wind noise is kept to a minimum. In fact, it is impossible not to make a comparison with the original Karmann-built Beetle cabriolet, the main difference being that the rear windshield is currently plastic, rather than glass. The Straman conversion is available with either a manual or fully electric top, the latter being especially impressive as it can be raised in around eight seconds and lowered in just six, all at the push of a button located in the center console.

The side profile is slightly different to the sedan's, with a higher roofline at the rear, but this

has been done to both offer greater headroom for rear-seat passengers and to reflect the style of the original Karmann-built Beetle cabriolet.

As one might expect, this is not an inexpensive conversion, with the manual-top model costing around $10,000 at the time of writing, and the power-operated model around $12,000—this is on top of the cost of a New Beetle saloon, of course. Not cheap, but what price style? The Straman Company requires your car for a maximum of three weeks, although Richard generally reckons that the conversion can be carried out in two. As Richard says, just imagine: You could soon be accelerating from zero to sun in six seconds and driving at 110 smiles per hour!

And wasn't the New Beetle built to put a smile on your face?

A protective "bra" from Colgan helps to prevent paint damage from stones out on the freeway. Its two-piece design means the hood can be opened without having to remove the bra first. *New Dimensions*

The New Beetle is an extremely aerodynamic vehicle, with a body design honed in a wind tunnel and checked by computer. However, among the first aftermarket products to become available were rear wings, or spoilers. Installation requires no more than a drill, simple hand tools and a free Sunday morning. We show you how we fitted a wing to our New Beetle—now it's your turn!

1. Start by holding up the wing to the trunk lid, making doubly sure that it is aligned perfectly with the lower edge of the rear window. *Author*

2. Also, check that the wing is placed symmetrically. Measure from the wing mounting to the edge of the trunk lid to be sure. *Author*

3. This particular wing uses a small central mounting post, which rests on the trunk lid above the factory third brake light. Other designs use the brake light fitting as a mounting point. *Author*

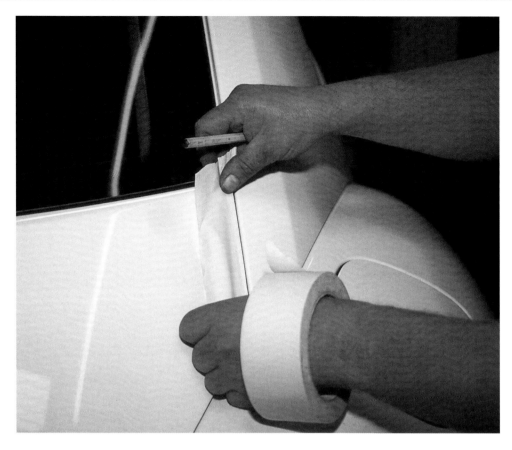

4. Use masking tape to protect the paintwork and to give a surface on which you can mark the position of the wing with a pen. *Author*

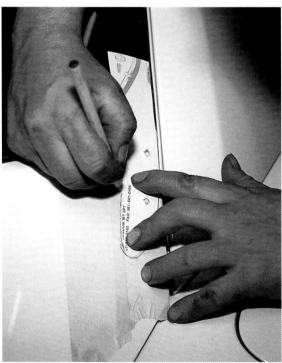

5. Some wings require that mounting holes be drilled in the trunk lid. If this is the case, the kit will almost certainly provide a template to show you where to drill the panel. *Author*

6. Use a spring-loaded center punch to mark the panel prior to drilling. You might want to double-check your dimensions before proceeding. *Author*

7. Start by drilling a pilot hole with a sharp drill bit. Set your drill on a slow speed to prevent the risk of the drill skidding on the panel and damaging the surrounding paint. *Author*

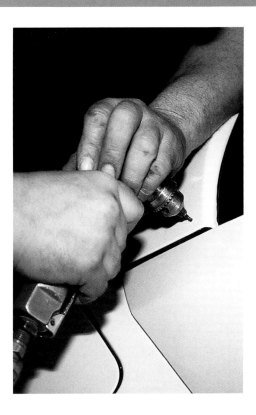

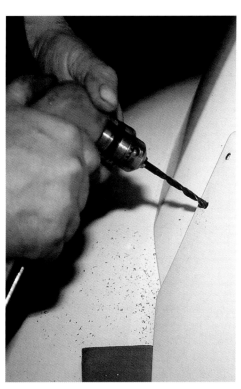

8. Now enlarge the holes, using a drill bit that matches the diameter of the mounting screws. Again, take your time and use a slow drilling speed. *Author*

9. Hopefully, this is what the job will look like from the top. Deburr the holes, using a small file or machinist's deburring tool. *Author*

10. The mounting holes end up being very close to the double-skinning on the tailgate, as can be seen from below. This is why it is so important to make sure that the wing is absolutely symmetrical. *Author*

11. Use a small brush to paint around the holes to stop them from rusting. Don't forget to do the underside as well. *Author*

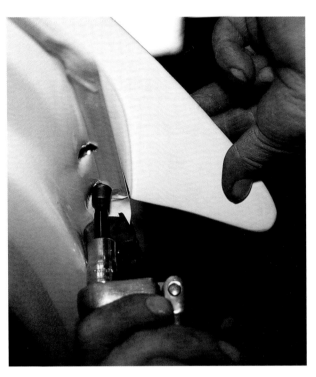

12. Install the mounting screws from below, and loosely bolt the wing in place. Take a look from the top and check that it is level before fully tightening the screws. *Author*

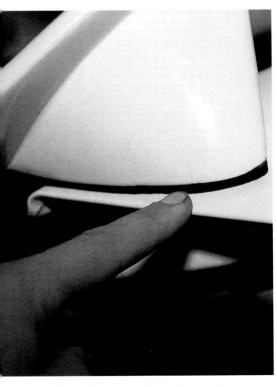

...nany cases, there will be a soft rubber gasket that fits between ...wing and the bodywork. If this is the case, don't forget to ...tall it before you fit the wing! *Author*

14. Job done! With the wing color matched to the car, it looks like a factory fitment. It's simple, smart, and functional. *Author*

The hottest style in Europe is what has become known as the DTM look, emulating the mighty racing sedans competing in the German touring car championship. To give your New Beetle the hot DTM style, we show you how to install a pair of front "splitters" to the factory front airdam. Once again, all you need are basic hand tools and a few minutes of your spare time—but the results are impressive!

European DTM-style front "splitters," or winglets, give the New Beetle a sporting look. They are easy to fit, and they help to change the whole character of the car. *Author*

1. The winglets are installed using one of the stock apron mounting screws on each side. They come predrilled, to make installation a cinch. *Author*

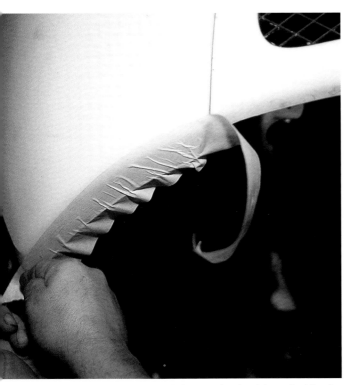

2. As you will need to drill one hole on each side of the underside of the apron, use masking tape to protect the paint and make it easier to mark drill holes. *Author*

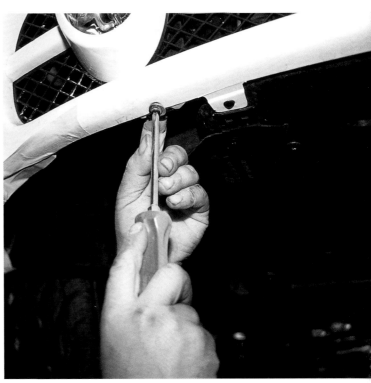

3. Remove the original factory mounting screw, but keep it safe, as you will use it when you install the winglet. *Author*

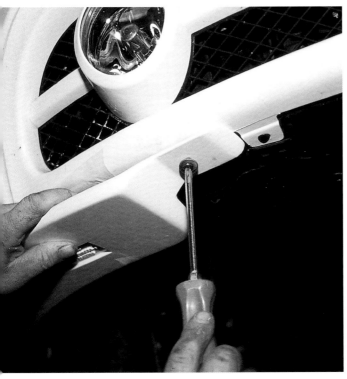

4. Hold the winglet up and loosely install it with the mounting screw you have just removed. Don't tighten it at this stage, as you will need to make some adjustments. *Author*

5. Looking from the side of the car, move the winglet until its rear edge aligns with the front edge of the fender. This will help to give the installation a professional look. *Author*

6. Once you are happy with the position of the winglet, use a piece of scrap (we used foam) to check the gap between the wing and the fender. This can then be used on the other side of the car to keep things symmetrical. *Author*

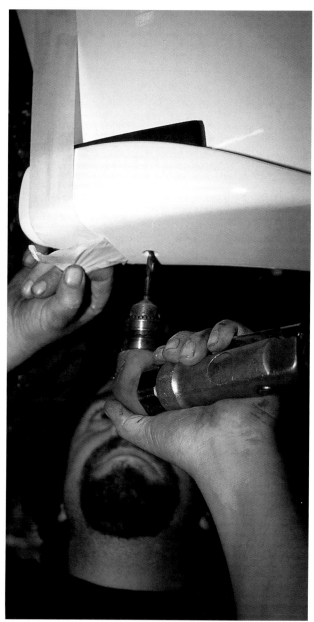

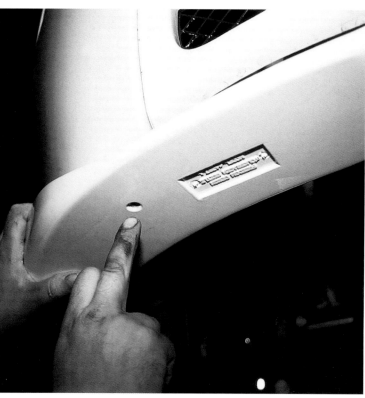

8. Drill the mounting hole, using a sharp drill bit. You won't need to use much effort, as you are only drilling into plastic. Note the tape used to support the winglet while you are drilling. *Author*

7. This is one of two other mounting holes on each winglet. Use a fine drill or sharp scriber to mark the position on the underside of the apron. *Author*

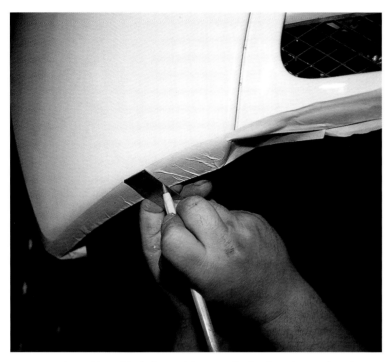

9. Measure the position of the holes, and then transfer the dimensions to the other side of the apron to make sure the winglets are placed symmetrically. *Author*

10. All that's left is to install the mounting screws supplied with the kit. Don't overtighten, as the plastic apron is quite soft. *Author*

11. Completed installation looks good. Color-code the winglets to match the bodywork for the factory look. *Author*

Chapter 7

Interiors

Color-coding the stock dashboard to match the exterior paintwork is a simple but dramatic way to dress up the interior. Bernt V1 project car's dash certainly hits you between the eyes. *Super GTI Magazine*

There is an old saying that beauty is only skin deep but, in the case of the New Beetle, this isn't so. Step behind the wheel of a New Beetle and you cannot fail to be impressed by the amount of thought that has gone into the design of the dashboard, instrumentation, steering wheel, and the interior fittings as a whole.

The dashboard is intentionally reminiscent of that found in the original VW Beetle, with a large round speedometer mounted directly in front of the driver. There are other design references to the old Bug, too, such as the grab handle mounted on the dashboard in front of the passenger seat or the elasticized map-pockets in the door—and even a

factory-fitted flower vase! Rear-seat passengers don't get left out, either, with door-pillar-mounted grab-handles that make getting into and out of the back seat far easier.

The steering wheel bears little resemblance to any that was ever fitted in an old Bug, largely because modern safety regulations mean that a driver air bag must be incorporated into the central hub. However, even this has been styled in such a way that it looks like a fun object, with chunky padded rim, aluminum-effect spokes, and a large VW logo in the center. This same chunky theme is carried through to the center console—a luxury that was never featured in the original Beetle—which

Stock seats are fine, if a little unexciting. Retrimming in leather will make a big difference to the look and feel of the interior, and may not be as costly as you think. *Author*

The interior of the ABD 1.8 Turbo project New Beetle looks superb retrimmed in duo-tone leather. Choose the colors carefully so they complement the exterior. *Author*

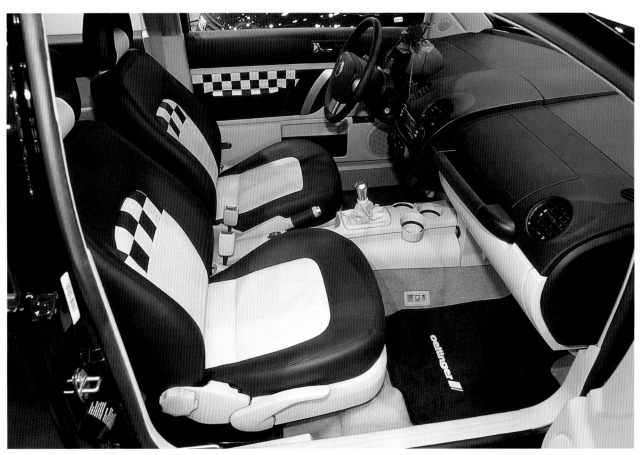

Here's a neat idea: Using a checkered-flag design on the seats and door trims gives the interior of this Oettinger-prepared New Beetle a sporting look. *Super GTI Magazine*

Swapping seats from another car in the VW lineup is a simple way to change the whole character of your New Beetle. Golf 4 GTi seats look great in this car from New RS Car in Belgium. *Super GTI Magazine*

houses controls for the heater and, if fitted, air conditioning, as well as the purpose-made stereo system. Below these is a useful cup holder for those who wish to enjoy their breakfast on the move and an electric socket for use with accessories such as a cellular phone. The one thing you won't find is an ashtray or a cigarette lighter—this is, after all, an eco-friendly car.

Probably the most striking aspect of the dashboard is its depth from the instrument binnacle forward to the base of the windshield. This is a consequence of the exterior styling of the New Beetle where, in side profile, the windshield pillars extend all the way forward to line up level with the front wheels. The effect inside the car is to give a tremendous feeling of space, and the view from the driver seat is similar to what one might expect in a small MPV. This sense of spaciousness is further reinforced by the high domed roofline and large glass area. Unfortunately, this same feeling of airiness isn't shared by rear-seat passengers, most of whom soon become accustomed to banging their heads against the substantial—and unpadded—rear windshield pillars each time the car goes round a sharp bend.

The New Beetle's seats are best described as comfortable and adequate, rather than ultrastylish. They are rounded in form to reflect the exterior design but they are not the most supportive of seats and a far cry from the Recaro-style seating of the more sporting Golf and Jetta models. In their favor is the fact that they slide forward and up when tilted, allowing easy access to the rear seat. The stock trim package revolves around cloth seat upholstery, with more luxurious leather as an option.

There is no reason why any number of aftermarket seats cannot be fitted to a New Beetle, although it is rare to see such a modification made. Companies such as Germany's Recaro produce sports seats of exceptionally high quality, some of which feature electric adjustment and even built-in heating, like the seating offered as part of the optional factory "winter package." By far the most popular custom seat upgrade is to have the stock seats reupholstered in leather or a high-quality leather-substitute material. Such retrims are not as costly as you might think, and it is definitely worth contacting a few auto upholstery businesses in your area to get a quote. If you are tempted, then always ask to examine examples of the company's handiwork before committing yourself.

Numerous products have been introduced onto the aftermarket to upgrade the interior of the New Beetle. Some, like the many designs of a bud vase currently on offer, are whimsical in their design. In fact, it is possible to replace the original clear plastic flower vase with anything from vintage-style ceramic vases right up to a range of high-tech CNC-machined billet-aluminum items. There is

How about this for a trick way to dress up the stock seats? Stitching VW logos into the backrests is very effective. *Dean Kirsten*

How wild do you want to go? The leopard-spot interior in WWF wrestling star Hulk Hogan's New Beetle is, to say the least, eye-catching! *Dean Kirsten*

Of course, you can always do away with the rear seats altogether, as in VW's own Dune styling exercise. Retrim the front seats in neoprene for the full "all-weather" effect! *Volkswagen*

This neat armrest from New Dimensions is a useful accessory, which makes long-distance driving a pleasure. Trimmed to match the rest of the interior, it almost looks like an original fitment. *New Dimensions*

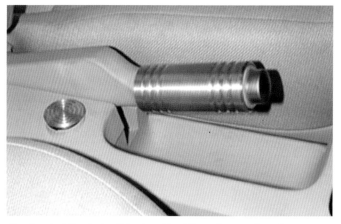

Carrying the billet-look still further, New Dimensions markets these two simple add-ons: covers for the emergency brake and electrics socket. *New Dimensions*

also a variety of special mountings to hold the vases. Although they are little more than cosmetic, these accessories are a fun way to brighten up the interior still further.

One of the more useful accessories you can buy to dress up the interior is the combined armrest and cup holder from New Dimensions. This neat unit, which can be easily installed by the owner, features a padded top cushion, some 10 inches long, that can be slid forward and backward

almost 4 inches to suit an individual's driving position. The rest, which is supported on aluminum-alloy mountings, incorporates a cup holder. This is slightly larger than the stock New Beetle holder, which is slightly too small to securely accommodate many drinking cups—especially those favored by most drive-through restaurants! Normally finished in black, ivory, or gray-grained vinyl to match the factory New Beetle trim options, the New Dimensions armrest is also

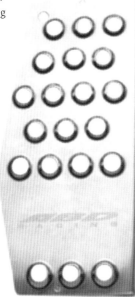

ABD's aluminum footrest is punched full of holes for that race car look. A must for the sporting New Beetle! *Autobahn Designs*

available to order trimmed in leather to suit custom retrims.

Billet accessories—some in aluminum, others in stainless steel—add a touch of high-tech class to any New Beetle interior. Sill plates, emergency brake handles, lower dash panels, and door lock buttons are all available in machined aluminum as direct replacements for the original factory pieces—not only long-lasting, they also completely change the character of the New Beetle's interior by turning the original retro-styling into something ultramodern. Installation of these is generally very straightforward, with no drilling required. The sill plates, for example, are normally held in place with a self-adhesive tape backing, while the door lock pulls simply screw in place once the originals have been removed.

For those wishing to give their car a more sporting look, several designs of foot-pedal covers are available, most in aluminum and drilled to give the appearance of a lightweight race car component. Installation will take only a few minutes but the effect is quite striking. These covers also have the added benefit of preventing wet feet slipping off the pedals. Matching aluminum

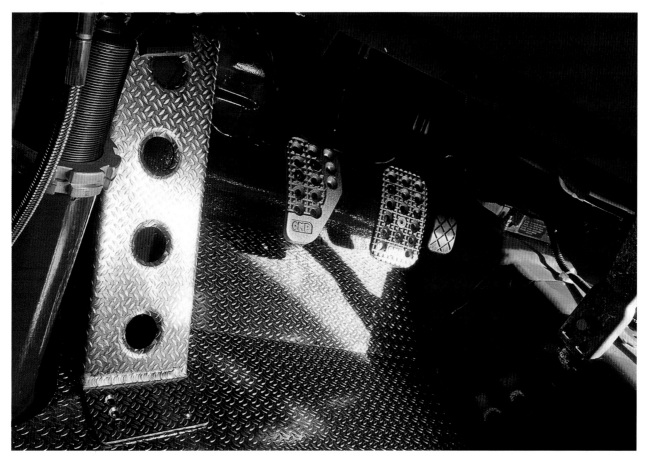

This is what the pedal assembly in a New Beetle Cup race car looks like. It wouldn't be that hard to duplicate in your street car for a no-nonsense look. *Super GTI Magazine*

ABD's sill cover carries the company logo and would be a stylish, yet practical, addition to any car. *Autobahn Designs*

An easy and effective way to dress up the stock dashboard is to use one of these German-made plastic covers, which simply slip over the top of the original dash. *New Dimensions*

footrests are also available to fit alongside the clutch pedal.

The perfect complement to the billet accessories would be one of the many self-adhesive dashboard decor kits. These are available in a wide variety of styles to change the appearance of your New Beetle's dashboard—it is possible to give your dash the appearance of being made from anything from carbon-fiber to aluminum, black marble, or even burled walnut. Kits vary in terms of the number of pieces supplied, some having as few as 12 components, others as many as 26, and include trim pieces for doors, window switches, and the radio fascia. The most expensive deco kits are those manufactured from genuine carbon fiber (as opposed to carbon-look material) or real wood. However, as the old saying goes, you only get what you pay for, so beware of kits that seem like a real bargain but end up peeling off the dash at the first sign of hot weather.

Installation of these kits is well within the capabilities of the average enthusiast, but it is imperative that the original dashboard surfaces are scrupulously clean and free from any silicones or grease. As each piece is ready-cut to the exact required shape, all that is necessary is to remove the paper backing from the self-adhesive surfaces and carefully locate in position before pushing firmly into place. That's all there is to it—an hour or two spent installing one of the many deco kits on the market will give your New Beetle interior a whole new look for a relatively small financial outlay. Such kits are available from a number of sources, including TVA and New Dimensions and have proved to be extremely popular.

As an alternative to this, New Dimensions also markets a one-piece cover that slips over the top of the central binnacle on the dashboard surrounding the radio, fresh-air vents, and heater controls. Quick and easy to install, these covers are available in nine different finishes, ranging from bright yellow to aluminum- and carbon-look.

One of the more striking aspects of the New Beetle at night is the soft blue lighting used to illuminate the instrumentation and switch gear. By day, however, the speedometer looks just like any other. Just think: you've fitted out the interior

The dashboard of New Dimensions' project car features this aluminum trim, which looks very high-tech without detracting from the style of the original. *New Dimensions*

with billet accessories, your dashboard now has the full carbon-effect look, and your seats are trimmed in soft gray leather—suddenly those gauges look very ordinary. So what's the answer? Maybe a replacement gauge face in white? Screen-printed onto thin plastic, these gauge faces can be installed in place of the factory original and come with either red or blue lettering. Although, due to the delicate nature of the speedometer needle, installation is something you may prefer to leave to the professionals, gauge faces are a quick and stylish way to brighten up the look of your dashboard.

One of the problems faced by the owner wishing to install accessory gauges is that there is precious little space available for them in, on, or around the dashboard of the New Beetle. The answer is to fit one of the dash-top gauge housings offered by a number of companies; they house three aftermarket instruments in a neat black or carbon-look casing. Angling the gauges toward the driver, this is a great way to give your New Beetle the race car look, and installation is simple. Wiring the gauges themselves—usually water temperature, oil pressure, and oil temperature—may be something you would prefer to leave to a

Autobahn Designs installed one of its gauge pods on top of the stock dashboard to allow the use of a group of aftermarket instruments. Installation looks almost "factory-original." *Author*

The carbon-fiber dash pod from Dietrich in Germany houses a single extra instrument, in this case a VDO oil temperature gauge. *Super GTI Magazine*

Although the stock speedometer looks very attractive, you may still feel the need to dress it up. If that's the case, then how about fitting one of these white face kits? *New Dimensions*

New Dimensions offers this practical and fun trunk mat with New Beetle logo stitched in. *New Dimensions*

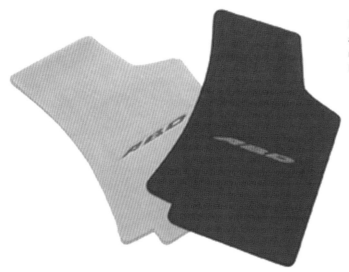

Protect the interior of your car—and add a dash of style—with a set of quality floor mats, such as these from Autobahn Designs. *Autobahn Designs*

The design of the New Beetle's dashboard precludes the use of a conventional DIN-sized stereo unit—unless you use one of Scosche's neat mounting adapters. *Scosche Industries*

professional auto-electrician, although it is not by any means beyond the capabilities of a good home mechanic.

Because the air bag is located in the center hub of the steering wheel, aftermarket wheels for modern vehicles are relatively few and far between. However, that need not be a problem for the New Beetle owner as there is an alternative: a Wheelskin. Made from soft leather, these self-fit covers are

handcrafted in California and feature a patented lacing system, which means that, when fitted, they are virtually indistinguishable from a genuine custom-made leather-bound steering wheel. They are available in a variety of colors—including two-tone designs—and can be complemented by matching shift knobs and lever gaiters (boots).

Due to the unique shape of the factory-fitted radio in the New Beetle, installing an aftermarket

ABD's trunk mat features the company logo. Stylish and functional, it helps to protect the trunk floor from damage. *Author*

hi-fi system isn't the straightforward proposition it might be with any other car. But help is at hand in the form of special adapter plates, such as Scosche Industries' Volkswagen radio fitting kit, Code Number VW2310. This fits into the factory radio slot in the dashboard in place of the original radio and has the regular so-called DIN-sized slot, which accepts virtually all aftermarket stereo header units. To accompany this is a wiring harness connector, to enable the new radio to integrate with the factory electrical system, and an adapter for use with the VW-fitted radio antenna.

Of more practical use is a set of heavy-duty floor mats and trunk liners. These might not seem very exciting products to mention in a performance handbook, but it is a fact of life that the more a car gets driven the more the interior will start to look shabby. If you build yourself a slick-handling, asphalt-eating New Beetle, the chances are you'll want to drive it far and often, no matter the weather. It won't be long before your carpets will start to look far from their best, and the answer here is to slip in a set of molded rubber mats before you go on that drive through the mountains. Similarly, if you enjoy such pursuits as skiing or snow-boarding, then the chances are your trunk will start to look rather well-used unless you take precautions to protect it from dirt and grime.

Many suppliers offer custom-made trunk carpets to help here, some of which feature attractive New Beetle or VW logos. Also of very practical use are custom-fit dashboard covers,

Ever wondered how to fit a mega-watt hi-fi system in a New Beetle? Well, here's one solution—as long as you don't want to carry anything in the trunk! *Super GTI Magazine*

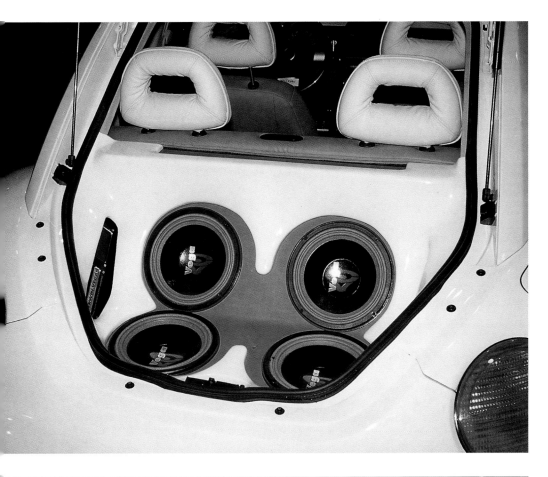

Bass speakers fill the trunk of this show car. The system probably produces more power than the engine. *Super GTI Magazine*

If you want some inspiration before restyling the interior of your New Beetle, look no further than the amazing dashboard of the original RSi styling exercise. Billet-aluminum center console and gear shift are just two ideas that could be put into practice. *Dean Kirsten*

The dashboard of the production version of the New Beetle RSi is somewhat more restrained but still looks stunning. Don't forget, all parts will eventually be available through your local VW dealership's parts department . . . at a price. *Volkswagen*

Volkswagen's Dune design exercise has many neat features that could be incorporated in a custom New Beetle. Check the floor and dash detailing for some ideas. *Volkswagen*

New Beetle Cup race cars feature Recaro seats and full roll cage for driver safety. Maybe a little spartan for road use but still very stylish. *Super GTI Magazine*

designed to protect the top of the dash from the effects of the sun's rays. Anyone who lives in a hot climate, such as southern California or Arizona, will appreciate how much damage the sun can do to a plastic dashboard. By fitting one of these covers, the risk of the dash top splitting or becoming discolored is greatly reduced.

How far you want to go with the interior of your New Beetle is, of course, a matter of personal taste and the size of your budget. The one thing you would be advised to do before embarking on a revamp of your car's interior is to give some thought to the overall style you are trying to achieve. Many of the New Beetles that were customized soon after their release onto the market looked a little like mobile Christmas trees, with every conceivable accessory bolted on in an attempt to personalize the car.

That's fine if that's the look you're after, but maybe it would be wise to sit back, take stock, and plan ahead. If, for example, you have given your car the "retro" look on the outside, with one of Kamei's body accessory kits and a set of vintage-style stoneguards, then do you really think a high-tech carbon-fiber dashboard and ultramodern billet-aluminum interior accessories are the way to go? Similarly, does a ceramic bud vase really look right in your slammed street-racer?

The New Beetle is such an amazing car, with so much thought having gone into every detail of its design, doesn't it deserve a few minutes' thought on your behalf before you try to change its character? And remember—whatever you decide to do to the interior, you'll be looking at it every time you step inside to take a ride. Sometimes a little self-restraint can go a long way.

It is still possible to install a roll cage and retain the original dashboard, as proved in this New Beetle spotted at a Las Vegas VW show. *Author*

If you don't mind dispensing with the radio, you can use the space to fit extra gauges, as on this New Beetle Cup car. *Super GTI Magazine*

And, of course, you can always brighten up the dashboard with an air-brushed mural. Individuality, that's what it's all about. *Author*

Specifications 2.0

Kercher-equipped New Beetle looks wild with its over-the-top rear spoiler. Four-tip exhaust system gives the car a purposeful look. *Super GTI Magazine*

New Beetle 2.0 GLS Technical Specifications

Engine

Type	1.8-liter, four-cylinder, inline	
Bore	3.25 inches	82.5 millimeters
Stroke	3.65 inches	92.8 millimeters
Displacement	121.0 inches (cubic)	1,984 cm (cubic)
Compression Ratio	10.0: 1	
Horsepower (SAE) @ rpm	115 @ 5,200	(85 kW @ 5,200)
Max. torque, ft-lb @ rpm	122 @ 2,600	(170 Nm @ 2,600)
0–60 mph	Manual 10.2 seconds	Automatic 11.5 seconds
Fuel Requirement	Regular unleaded	

Engine Design

Arrangement	Front-mounted, transverse
Cylinder Block	Cast-iron
Crankshaft	Cast-iron, five main bearings
Cylinder Head	Aluminum alloy, cross-flow
Valvetrain	Single overhead camshaft, spur-belt driven, two valves per cylinder, maintenance-free hydraulic lifters, single-coil valve springs
Cooling System	Water-cooled, water pump, cross-flow radiator, thermostatically controlled electric two-speed radiator fan
Lubrication	Rotary gear pump, chain-driven from crankshaft, oil cooler
Fuel/Air Supply	Sequential multipoint fuel injection (Motronic)
Emissions	OBD II, LEV, three-way catalytic converter with two oxygen sensors, onboard refueling vapor recovery (ORVR). California cars with secondary air-pump.

Volkswagen made everybody sit up and take notice when the Dune concept car was first shown in 1999. Who will be the first to build a New Beetle off-road vehicle?
Volkswagen

Electrical System

Alternator, Volts/Amps	14/90
Battery, Volts (Amp Hours)	12 (60)
Ignition	Digital electronic with knock sensor
Firing Order	1-3-4-2

Specifications 2.0

This view from above shows off the Dune's amazing full-length sunroof. Think how cool it would be to cruise down Pacific Coast Highway in this! *Volkswagen*

Drivetrain

Drivetrain	Front-wheel-drive						
Gear Ratios	1st	2nd	3rd	4th	5th	Reverse	Final
Manual	3.78:1	2.12:1	1.36:1	1.03:1	0.84:1	3.06:1	4.24:1
Automatic	2.71:1	1.55:1	1.00:1	0.68:1	N.A.	2.11:1	4.88:1

Capacities

Engine Oil (with filter)	4.2 quarts (U.S.)	4.0 liters
Fuel Tank	14.5 gallons (U.S.)	55.0 liters
Coolant System	6.7 quarts (U.S.)	6.3 liters
Wiper Fluid	2.1 quarts (U.S.)	2.0 liters

Steering

Type	Rack-and-pinion, power-assisted
Turns (lock to lock)	3.2
Turning Circle	32.8 feet (10.0 meters)
Ratio	17.8: 1

Interior Volumes

EPA	Sub-Compact	
Passenger Volume	81 feet (cubic)	2.3 meters (cubic)
Trunk Volume	12 feet (cubic)	0.3 meters (cubic)
Seating Capacity	four	

Body, Chassis, and Suspension

Type	Unitized construction, bolt-on front and rear fenders
Front Suspension	Independent MacPherson struts, coil springs, telescopic shock absorbers, stabilizer bar
Rear Suspension	Independent torsion beam axle, coil springs, telescopic shock absorbers, stabilizer bar
Brakes	Power-assisted, dual-circuit, vented 280-mmx22-mm front discs and 232-mmx9-mm solid rear discs
Anti-lock Braking System	Standard, all four wheels
Parking Brake	Mechanical, effective on rear wheels
Wheels	6-1/2 Jx16 steel (alloy wheels optional)
Tires	P205/55 R16H all-weather tires
Drag Coefficient	0.38

Exterior Dimensions

Wheelbase	98.9 inches	2,512 millimeters
Front Track	59.6 inches	1,514 millimeters
Rear Track	58.7 inches	1,491 millimeters
Length	161.1 inches	4,092 millimeters
Width	67.9 inches	1,725 millimeters
Height	59.5 inches	1,511 millimeters
Ground Clearance	4.2 inches	107 millimeters

Weights

Curb Weight

Manual Transmission	2,785 pounds	1,283 kilograms
Automatic Transmission	2,833 pounds	1,305 kilograms

Payload

Manual Transmission	860 pounds	390 kilograms
Automatic Transmission	860 pounds	390 kilograms

Okay, so it's not as wild as the Dune, but New Dimensions' "Purple HaZe" project car still looks right at home on the beach. But where's the surfboard? *New Dimensions*

Fuel Consumption

City	mpg	L/100 km
Manual Transmission	24	9.8
Automatic Transmission	22	10.5
Highway	mpg	L/100 km
Manual Transmission	31	7.0
Automatic Transmission	28	7.6

Specifications 1.8T

New Beetle 1.8 Turbo GLX Technical Specifications

Engine

Type	Four-cylinder, inline	
Bore	3.19 inches	81.0 millimeters
Stroke	3.40 inches	86.4 millimeters
Displacement	108.6 inches (cubic)	1,781 cm (cubic)
Compression Ratio	9.5:1	
Horsepower (SAE) @ rpm	150 @ 5,800	(110kW @ 5,800)
Max. torque, ft-lb @ rpm	162 @ 2,200–4,200	(220Nm @ 2,200–4,200)
0-60 mph	Manual 8.2 seconds	Automatic 9 seconds
Fuel Requirement	Premium unleaded (91)	

Engine Design

Arrangement	Front-mounted, transverse
Cylinder Block	Cast-iron
Crankshaft	Forged steel, five main bearings
Cylinder Head	Aluminum alloy, cross-flow
Valvetrain	Double overhead camshaft, spur-belt driven, five valves per cylinder, maintenance-free hydraulic lifters
Cooling System	Water-cooled, water pump, cross-flow radiator, thermostatically controlled electric radiator fan
Lubrication	Rotary gear pump, chain-driven, oil cooler
Fuel/Air Supply	Sequential multipoint fuel injection (ME 7.1), turbocharger
Emissions	OBD II, TLEV, three-way catalytic converter with two oxygen sensors, onboard refueling vapor recovery (ORVR)

Want to head for the mountains? With an adapter, PIP's roofrack can be transformed into a bike carrier. *New Dimensions*

Did you say "bright"? Bernt's own project car is as about "in your face" as you can get. Pearlescent orange paintwork makes this New Bug really stand out. *Super GTI Magazine*

Specifications 1.8T

Fat fenders allow wide rims and radically lowered suspension to work together. Normally, when a car is this low, you start running into fender clearance problems. *Super GTI Magazine*

Electrical System

Alternator, Volts/Amps	14/90
Battery, Volts (Amp Hours)	12 (60)
Ignition	Digital electronic with knock sensor
Firing Order	1-3-4-2

Drive Train

Drive Train   Front-Wheel-Drive

Gear Ratios	1st	2nd	3rd	4th	5th	Reverse	Final
Manual	3.30:1	1.94:1	1.31:1	1.03:1	0.84:1	3.06:1	3.94:1
Automatic	2.71:1	1.44:1	1.00:1	0.74:1	N.A.	2.881	4.43:1

Capacities

Engine Oil (with filter)	4.8 quarts (U.S.)	4.5 liters
Fuel Tank	14.5 gallons (U.S.)	55.0 liters
Coolant System	6.7 quarts (U.S.)	6.3 liters
Wiper Fluid	2.1 quarts (U.S.)	2.0 liters

Steering

Type	Rack-and-pinion, power-assisted
Turns (lock to lock)	3.2
Turning Circle	32.8 feet (10.0 meters)
Ratio	17.8:1

Interior Volumes

EPA	Sub-Compact	
Passenger Volume	81 feet (cubic)	2.3 meters (cubic)
Trunk Volume	12 feet (cubic)	0.3 meters (cubic)
Seating Capacity	four	

Body, Chassis, and Suspension

Type	Unitized construction, bolt-on front and rear fenders
Front Suspension	Independent MacPherson struts, coil springs, telescopic shock absorbers, stabilizer bar
Rear Suspension	Independent torsion beam axle, coil springs, telescopic shock absorbers, stabilizer bar
Brakes	Power-assisted, dual-circuit, vented 280-mmx22-mm front discs and 232-mmx9-mm solid rear discs
Anti-lock Braking System	Standard, all four wheels
Parking Brake	Mechanical, effective on rear wheels
Wheels	6-1/2 Jx16 alloy
Tires	P205/55 R 16 H all-weather tires
Drag Coefficient	0.38

Exterior Dimensions

Wheelbase	98.9 inches	2,512 millimeters
Front Track	59.6 inches	1,514 millimeters
Rear Track	58.7 inches	1,491 millimeters
Length	161.1 inches	4,092 millimeters
Width	67.9 inches	1,725 millimeters
Height	59.5 inches	1,511 millimeters
Ground Clearance	4.2 inches	107 millimeters

Weights

Curb Weight

Manual Transmission	2,964 pounds	1.322 kilograms
Automatic Transmission	3,008 pounds	1.342 kilograms

Payload

Manual Transmission	860 pounds	390 kilograms
Automatic Transmission	860 pounds	390 kilograms

Fuel Consumption

City	*mpg*	*L/100 km*
Manual Transmission	24	9.7
Automatic Transmission	22	10.7
Highway	mpg	L/100 km
Manual Transmission	31	7.0
Automatic Transmission	28	7.8

Cesam's project car has more than a hint of the classic Porsche Carrera, with its reversed-out graphics and ice-white paintwork.
Super GTI Magazine

Budnik manufactures a wide range of billet aftermarket wheels for all kinds of car. Directional wheels look especially good on the New Beetle.
Super GTI Magazine

Specifications 1.9

Carrera-Bug sits slightly nose down for a hot-rod look, which suits the New Beetle well. Bodywork is all stock, but red detailing gives the car a whole new style. *Super GTI Magazine*

New Beetle 1.9 TDI GLS Technical Specifications

Engine

Type	1.9-liter, four-cylinder inline turbocharged direct-injection diesel	
Bore	3.13 inches	79.5 millimeters
Stroke	3.76 inches	95.5 millimeters
Displacement	121.0 inches (cubic)	1,896 cm (cubic)
Compression Ratio	19.5: 1	
Horsepower (SAE) @ rpm	90 @ 3,750	(66kW @ 3,750)
Max. torque, ft-lb @ rpm	155 @ 1,900	(2,10Nm @ 1,900)
0–60 mph	Manual 11.9 seconds	Automatic 14.1 seconds
Fuel Requirement	Diesel	

Engine Design

Arrangement	Front-mounted, transverse
Cylinder Block	Cast-iron
Crankshaft	Cast-iron, five main bearings
Cylinder Head	Aluminum alloy, cross-flow
Valvetrain	Single overhead camshaft, spur-belt driven, two valves per cylinder, maintenance-free hydraulic lifters, single-coil valve springs
Cooling System	Water-cooled, water pump, cross-flow radiator, thermostatically controlled electric three-speed radiator fan
Lubrication	Rotary gear pump, intermediate-shaft driven, oil cooler
Fuel/Air Supply	Electronically controlled direct-injection (EDC), turbocharger
Emissions	OBD D, Tier 1, catalytic converter, water-cooled EGR system, onboard refueling vapor recovery (ORVR)

Electrical System

Alternator, Volts/Amps	14/90
Battery, Volts (Amp Hours)	12 (60)
Ignition	Compression ignition
Firing Order	1-3-4-2

Drive Train

Drive Train	Front-Wheel Drive						
Gear Ratios	1st	2nd	3rd	4th	5th	Reverse	Final
Manual	3.78:1	2.12:1	1.36:1	0.97:1	0.76:1	3.60:1	3.39:1
Automatic	2.71:1	1.44:1	1.00:1	0.74:1	N.A.	2.88:1	3.20:1

Capacities

Engine Oil (with filter)	4.8 quarts (U.S.)	4.5 liters
Fuel Tank	14.5 gallons (U.S.)	55.0 liters
Coolant System	5.5 quarts (U.S.)	5.2 liters
Wiper Fluid	3.2 quarts (U.S.)	3.0 liters

Specifications 1.9

Oettinger-prepared New Beetle wears sporty checkered paintwork for a new look. Beneath the hood lurks a 140-horsepower 2-liter gasoline motor. *Super GTI Magazine*

Steering

Type	Rack-and-pinion, power-assisted	
Turns (lock to lock)	3.2	
Turning Circle	32.8 feet (10.0 meters)	
Ratio	17.8:1	

Interior Volumes

EPA	Sub-Compact	
Passenger Volume	81 feet (cubic)	2.3 meters (cubic)
Trunk Volume	12 feet (cubic)	0.3 meters (cubic)
Seating Capacity	four	

Body, Chassis, and Suspension

Type	Unitized construction, bolt-on front and rear fenders
Front Suspension	Independent MacPherson struts, coil springs, telescopic shock absorbers, stabilizer bar
Rear Suspension	Independent torsion beam axle, coil springs, telescopic shock absorbers, stabilizer bar
Brakes	Power-assisted, dual-circuit, vented 280-mmx22-mm front discs and 232-mmx9-mm solid rear discs
Anti-lock Braking System	Standard, all four wheels
Parking Brake	Mechanical, effective on rear wheels
Wheels	6-1/2 Jx16 steel (alloy wheels optional)
Tires	P205/55 R16H all weather tires
Drag Coefficient	0.38

Bugster Unlimited is the company behind this crazy "speedster" conversion. Two-seat sportster features a hard tonneau cover and individual rollover bars. *Super GTI Magazine*

Exterior Dimensions

Wheelbase	98.9 inches	2,512 millimeters
Front Track	59.6 inches	1,514 millimeters
Rear Track	58.7 inches	1,491 millimeters
Length	161.1 inches	4,092 millimeters
Width	67.9 inches	1,725 millimeters
Height	59.5 inches	1,511 millimeters
Ground Clearance	4.2 inches	107 millimeters

Weights

Curb Weight

Manual Transmission	2,867 pounds	1,320 kilograms
Automatic Transmission	2,917 pounds	1,324 kilograms

Payload

Manual Transmission	860 pounds	390 kilograms
Automatic Transmission	860 pounds	390 kilograms

Fuel Consumption

City	mpg	L/100 km
Manual Transmission	42	5.6
Automatic Transmission	34	6.9
Highway	mpg	L/100 km
Manual Transmission	49	4.4
Automatic Transmission	45	4.8

New Beetle Specialists

Kamei, the long-established German accessory specialist, created this amazing New Beetle cabriolet to show off the company's range of extras. *Super GTI Magazine*

Abt Sportline GmbH
Daimlerstrasse 2
D-87437 Kempten/Allgaü
Germany
+49 (0)831-72666
www.der-abt.de
Bodystyling

Advanced Motorsport Solutions (AMS)
850 W 18th Street
Costa Mesa, California 92627
USA
(949) 515-1672
www.advancedmotorsport.com
Performance conversions

Autobahn Designs (ABD Racing)
2900 Adams Street
Suite B-27
Riverside, California 92504
USA
(909) 351-9575
www.abdracing.com
Performance and styling conversions

Autotech Sport tuning
32240-E Paseo Adelanto
San Juan Capistrano, California 92675
USA
(949) 240-4000
www.autotech.com
Quaife distributors USA

Beetlechoose
Theresienstrasse 17
D-90762 Fürth
Germany
+49 (0)91174-2933
www.beetlechoose.de
Performance and styling conversions

Bilstein
5828 Ennepetal 13
Postfach 1151
Germany
+49 (0)2333-7920
Suspension upgrades

The interior of Kamei's roadster is stunning. Kamei calls the car the Beetster—a cross between a Beetle and a Speedster! *Super GTI Magazine*

Dr. Boltz Motorsports
2699 Pacific Coast Highway
Hermosa Beach, California 90254
USA
(310) 318-3519
www.drboltz.com
Performance and styling conversions

Borla Performance Industries
5901 Edison Drive
Oxnard, California 93033
USA
(805) 986-8600
www.borla.com
Exhaust systems

Brembo Brakes
1585 Sunflower Avenue
Costa Mesa, California 92626
USA
(714) 641-0104
Braking upgrades

Bugpack (Prothane)
3560 Cadillac Avenue
Costa Mesa, California 92626
USA
(714) 979-4990
www.deeeng.com
Suspension upgrades

Beetleland
Les Rouardes
42320 Grand Croix
France
+33 (0)4-7773-6061
Performance and styling conversions

Bugster Unlimited
1831 Redondo Avenue
Signal Hill, California 90804
USA
(562) 986-9053
www.bugster.com
Roadster conversions

New Beetle Specialists

Not to be outdone, Beetles Revival shows how good a convertible New Beetle can look. This example has the style of the old air-cooled Beetle convertible. *Super GTI Magazine*

Carrera Shocks
5412 New Peachtree Road
Atlanta, Georgia 30341
USA
(770) 451-8811
www.carrerashocks.com
Suspension upgrades

Cesam
BP 76
69743 Genas
France
+33 (0)47279-0290
www.cesam.com
Performance and styling conversions

Classics by Bernt
8420 Katella Avenue
Stanton, California 90680
USA
(714) 527-8464
www.classicbybernt.com
Body styling and accessories

Dietrich
Merkureck 4a
D-48154 Münster-Hiltrup
Germany
+49 (0)25011-6660
Performance and styling conversions

Earl's Performance Products
189 West Victoria
Long Beach, California 90805
USA
(310) 609-1602
High-pressure hoses and fittings

Eibach Springs Inc
17817 Gillette Avenue
Irvine, California 92614-6501
USA
(949) 752-6700
www.eibach.com
Suspension products

Autobahn Designs was one of the first companies to build a custom New Beetle. Stunning in its original silver, the ABD Bug was subtle, yet stylish. *Author*

Flat-4 of Tokyo
6-36-7 Shimouma
Setagaya-Ku
154 Tokyo
Japan
+81 (0)3-3424-0510
Accessories and wheels

HPA Motorsports
101-5763 198th Street
Langley, British Columbia
V3A 1G5
Canada
(604) 530-3715
www.hpamotorsports.com
Performance conversions

H&R Special Springs (USA)
3815 Bakerview Spur, #7
Bellingham, Washington 98226
USA
(360) 738-8889
Suspension upgrades

H&R Spezialfedern
Elsper strasse 36
57368 Lennestadt
Germany
+49 (0)2721-92600
www.hr-spezialfedern.de
Suspension upgrades

H-S Motorsports
629 Millcroft Place
Waterloo, Ontario
N2T 2P4
Canada
(519) 570-3648
www.hsmotorsports.com
Performance conversions

K&N Engineering (USA)
PO Box 1329
Riverside, California 92502
USA
(909) 684-9762
Air filter upgrades

New Beetle Specialists

HPA Motorsports in Canada created one of the first VR6-engined New Beetles. The end result was a real street-sleeper, which must have caught many local musclecar owners unawares. *Dean Kirsten*

Kerscher
Eggenfeldenerstrasse 46a
D-84326 Falkenburg
Germany
+49 (0)87279-6880
Performance and styling conversions

Landspeed
300 West Paseo Redondo
Tucson, Arizona 85701
USA
(520) 882-9965
www.landspeedusa.com
Performance and styling conversions

Mintex Don Ltd
PO Box 18
Cleckheaton, West Yorkshire
BD19 3UJ
England
+44 (0)1274 878711
Brake pads

MLM
Lintorfer Waldstrasse 5
D-40489 Düsseldorf
Germany
+49 (0)20374-1412
Body styling

Momentum Motorsport
309-1952 Kingsway Avenue
Port Coquitlam, British Columbia
V3C 6C2
Canada
(604) 552-9707
www.momentummotor.com
Performance conversions

EMPI Mr. Bug, better known for its accessory range for air-cooled Bugs, got in on the New Beetle act with this striking machine. It pays homage to the original "Inch Pincher" VW drag race car of the 1970s. In the background is TVA's retro-looking New Beetle, complete with period-style accessories. *Author*

Neuspeed
3300 Corte Malpasso
Camarillo, California 93012
USA
(805) 388-7171
www.neuspeed.com
Performance conversions

New Dimensions
2240 De La Cruz Blvd
Santa Clara, California 95050
USA
(408) 980-1691
www.vwaftermarket.com
Performance and styling conversions

New RS Car
18 Quai Culot
5500 Dinant
Belgium
+32 (0)7572-8867
Performance and styling conversions

TVA car features a set of Flat-4 of Japan's BRM-style wheels for a vintage feel. These are replicas of magnesium wheels made for the old Bugs back in the late 1960s. *Author*

BRM-style wheels look especially good on a black car. Stoneguards and door-handle finger plates help with the nostalgic look. *Super GTI Magazine*

New Beetle Specialists

Porsche wheels, studded tires, and race car graphics—something's going on here. This is no ordinary New Beetle . . . . *Super GTI Magazine*

Hold on, where's the engine? Beneath the "hood" sits the gas tank—so what's happened to the drivetrain? *Super GTI Magazine*

Oettinger Technik GmbH
Max-Planckstrasse 36
D-61381 Freidrichsdorf
Germany
+49 (0)6172-95330
Performance and styling conversions

Projectzwo Automobildesign GmbH
Saarburgstrasse 13
D-868999 Landsberg/Lech
Germany
+49 (0)81-9192770
www.projektzwo.de
Body styling

R T Quaife Engineering Ltd
Vestry Road
Otford, Sevenoaks, Kent
TN14 5EL
England
+44 (0)1732 741144
www.quaife.co.uk
Transmission conversions

The Real Source
One Mid America Place
Effingham, Illinois 62401
USA
(217) 347-5591
www.800luvbugg.com
New Beetle Accessories

New Beetle Specialists

Schrick
Dreherstrasse 3-5
42899 Remscheid
Germany
+49 (0)2191-9500
Camshafts

Scosche Industries
1550 Pacific Avenue
Oxnard, California 93034
USA
(805) 486-4450
Radio fittings

Richard Straman Co
846 Production Place
Newport Beach, California 92663
USA
(949) 548-8515
Cabriolet conversions

Techtonics Tuning
PO Box 295
Sheridan, Oregon 97378
USA
(503) 843-2700
www.tttuning.com
Performance conversions

Inside, there are few clues as to what's going on. Maybe the Porsche instrumentation is a hint at what lies under the skin of this New Beetle?
Super GTI Magazine

New Beetle Specialists

The answer? With a tube chassis and a midmounted 3.5-liter Porsche 911 engine producing 340 horsepower, this particular New Beetle is built for ice racing in France! *Super GTI Magazine*

TVA
2781 Saturn Street, Unit A
Brea, California 92821
USA
(714) 792-3975
www.aiwana.com
New Beetle accessories

Velocity Sport Tuning
24418 S. Main Street, #404
Carson, California 90745
USA
(310) 952-0003
www.velocitysport.com
Performance conversions

The New Beetle Cup race series is very popular in Germany. Everyone loves to watch these factory-built VR6-engined race cars battle it out on the circuits of Europe. *Super GTI Magazine*

Volkswagen of America
3800 Hamlin Road
Auburn Hills, Michigan 48326
USA
(248) 340-5000
www.vw.com
New Beetle accessories

VW Specialties
17862 Gothard Street
Huntington Beach, California 92647
USA
(714) 848-3766
Performance conversions

Wetterauer America Inc
1150 Eastport Center Drive
Valparaiso, Indiana 46383
USA
(219) 477-6806
www.chip-tuning.com
Engine management systems

Publications
Hot VWs Magazine
Wright Publishing
PO Box 2260
2950 Airway A-7
Costa Mesa, California 92626
USA
(714) 979-2560
www.hotvws.com

VW Trends
2400 E Katella, 11th floor
Anaheim, California 92806
USA
(714) 939-2400
www.vwtrendsweb.com

European Car
2400 E Katella, 11th floor
Anaheim, California 92806
USA
(714) 939-2400
www.europeancarweb.com

VolksWorld
Focus House
Dingwall Avenue
Croydon, CR9 2TA
England
+44 (0)208 774 0660
www.volksworld.com

Each car in the New Beetle Cup series is very colorful, with colors including bright yellow, red, green, and blue. The radical aerodynamic package hints at the New Beetle RSi. *Super GTI Magazine*

VW Driver
Campion House
1 Greenfield Road
Westoning, Bedfordshire
MK45 5JD
England
+44 (0)1525 750500
www.autometrix.com

Super GTI Magazine
BP 18, Lege-Bourg
33950 Lege-Cap-Ferret
France
+33 (0)55603-9090
www.supergti.com

VW Speed
Am Sandfeld 4
76149 Karlsruhe
Germany
+49 (0)721-6273820

The ultimate New Beetle? This rear-engined drag racer was built by Ron Lummus and is powered by a nitrous oxide-injected flat-four motor. Nine-second quarter-miles are as easy as "ABC." *Author*

Index

A4 Platform, 21
Aerodymensions, 76, 79
Anderson, Dave, 37, 40, 53
Anti-lock braking (ABS), 21
AQY, 31–33
Autobahn Designs (ABD), 32, 37, 49, 52
Automatic Torque Biasing (ATB)
      differential, 43, 44
Autotech, 43
      Q-Chip, 37

Bilstein, 51, 53
Body-styling kits, 75
      Belgian RSD kit, 78
      Bolt-ons, 75
      Eyebrows, 75
      Finger plates, 75
      Projektzwo kit, 77
      Stone guards, 75, 79
      V1 kit, 76, 78, 79
Body panels, 75
Bodywork
      Colgan bra, 81
      Perfect Fit bra, 81
      Two-element rear-wing, 73
      Winging, 82–85
Bud Vase, 93
Brake discs, 46

Coefficient of drag, 27
Concept 1, 6, 7, 9–12, 72

Dashboard, 90
Dietrich, 79

Eaton M45 supercharger, 39
Engines
      1.5-liter four-cylinder inline unit,
        29
      1.6-liter, 25, 30
      1.8-liter turbo-charged gasoline,

        21, 24, 26, 27, 34–36, 40, 75
      1.9-liter turbo-diesel, 21, 23, 26,
        27, 31, 36, 37
      2.0-liter four cylinder, 21, 23, 26,
        31, 34, 36
      2.3-liter V5, 21, 24
      3.2-liter VR6, 21, 28, 41
Engine Control Unit (ECU), 33, 35–37, 40
Engine management system (EMS), 34
Exhaust Gas Recirculating (EGR), 36
Exhaust systems
      Autotech, 38, 40
      Borla Exhaust, 29
      Borla Tailpipes, 30
      Neuspeed, 38, 40
      Remus, 38
      Stock Exhaust, 29
      Supersprint, 38
      Techtonics Tuning, 38

Fenders, 72
Fuel gauge, 25

Garrett T3/T4 hybrid turbo system, 41
Grab-handle
      On dashboard, 25
      Rear, 22

Hildebrand, Tim, 37

Instrumentation, 90
Interiors, 90–103

Japan Motor Show, 12

K04 turbo kit, 35
Kamei, 75
KKK K03, 34, 35
Koni, 52

Mass Air Flow (MAF), 34, 35, 36

Mays, J. Carrol, 6, 7, 11, 12
Momentum Motorsport, 41

Neuspeed P-Flow air-filter system, 33, 37
Neuspeed's P-chip, 34, 37
New Beetle Rsi, 13, 18, 73
New Dimensions, 39, 40
Nitrous Express, 41
North American International Auto Show
        (1994), 6
NOS, 41

Quaife, 43

Race Brake Kit, 56
Recaro, 93

Secondary Air Injection Valve, 33
Speedometer, 25
Splitters, 76, 86–89
Spoiler, 76
Steering wheel, 90
Straman, Richard, 80
Suspension, Front,
        MacPherson strut front
          suspension, 21, 46, 47
        Upgrading, 58–64
Suspension, Rear,
        Torsion-beam axle, 46, 48
        Upgrading, 65–71

Tachometer, 25
Temperature gauge, 25
Thomas, Freeman, 6, 7, 11, 12
Transmission
        02J manual gearbox, 42, 43
        AG4 Phase II Eta transmission, 43
        Electronic transmission control
module (TCM), 43
        Five-speed manual, 42
        Four-speed fully automatic, 42
        Six-speed dog-engagement
          transmission, 45
Trunk, 26
Turbonetics, 41

Wetterauer, Frank, 37

Zender, 75

Also by Keith Seume

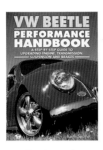

**VW Beetle
Performance Handbook**
ISBN: 0-7603-0469-6

**VW Beetle:
A New Custom Handbook**
ISBN: 0-7603-0622-2

**Millenium Bug:
A VW Scrapbook**
ISBN: 0-7603-0818-7

Other MBI Publishing Company titles of interest:

The New Beetle
ISBN: 0-7603-0644-3

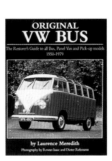

Original VW Bus
ISBN: 1-870979-84-2

**Illustrated Buyer's Guide:
Volkswagen, 2nd Edition**
ISBN: 0-7603-1162-5

**Original VW Beetle,
Updated Edtion**
ISBN: 0-901432-27-0

**Water-cooled
Volkswagen Performance
Handbook**
ISBN: 0-7603-0491-2

Find us on the internet at www.motorbooks.com   1-800-826-6600